JOSEPH

POSITIONED FOR PURPOSE

NATALIE BRECKENRIDGE

JOSEPH

POSITIONED FOR PURPOSE

Dedication

This work is dedicated to my precious and beautiful family. Everything I ever write will be with you in mind. I love you all more than words can ever say.

Contents

Introduction

What if the moments that we resist most are the moments that are positioning us for true purpose? What if the evil that had been thrown our way was, in fact, turned for our good? Oftentimes, we are binding the devil, loosing the Holy Ghost and waging war against dark forces in the heavenlies, only to feel as though nothing has changed. There can be many reasons for why things may remain the same in a season, and sometimes, that ends up being a very long season of warfare, but one clear truth remains; what was meant for evil, God is using for our good. Better yet, sometimes God is using these seasons for His own good.

We are being positioned for purpose. True purpose. God purpose. The kind of purpose that exposes the plots of hell for what they are and renders them useless. The kind of purpose that marks your life and vindicates your soul from the "what if", "should've" and "could've". If we are honest, most people do not fulfill their purpose. They live this life, passively, and just wander without a cause. How are there so many that surrender purpose on the altar of conformity, while there is measurable change at the hands of those who dare to get into position; those who have lived purposefully fulfilled lives and rocked our generations to the core?

These are the forerunners, the reformers and the agents of change that God uses on the earth. Could it be that they all have one thing in common? Could it be that if we look beyond the surface and dare to push past the outward appearance, we would find the same strength pushed them all?

If the answer is yes, (and I dare say that it is) then, what is this that causes others to rise while most retreat? If we could truly hone in on this, it could certainly be bottled and sold, right? The truth is simple and in plain sight, yet, only those with eyes to see and ears to hear will truly take hold of what is about to be spoken. Those forerunners, reformers, agents of change, etc. learned the power of pain and the prevailing truth that God can and will use ALL things. Their pain was real, they felt it and endured just like me and you, yet, when the moment was over, they breathed as though they had been given an assurance that even in the midst of their suffering, they could and would move forward in spite of it all.

Their pain became preparation and their setbacks became divine moments of positioning. What if all this time, you were being put in position for your purpose? What if? I dare you to believe the word of God. I dare you to think, with me, beyond the borders of your comfort. Let's explore the realms of God's truth that bring us endurance and birth the change that impacts generations. I dare you to commit to the truth that all that has happened in your life...all the good and exciting moments as well as the vile, demonic and evil that you have experienced...were positioning you for purpose.

John 10:10 says, "Jesus came to give you life and life more abundantly. Satan came to steal, kill and destroy." Our Father is good and He does not have to use evil to cause His great plans to come about, yet the truth remains in tact that God does use all things for the good of those who love Him. He uses all things. I will say it again! Let it sink down deep into your soul. He uses ALL things. What the enemy meant for evil, God turns around and uses for good. So, get ready for the ride of a lifetime as we study the life and story of Joseph, the son of Jacob. No matter where you sit on the spectrum of your life, I am confident you will find yourself relating deeply to Joseph. It is time for you to be positioned for purpose!

1

Birth in Betrayal

Then God remembered Rachel, and God listened to her and opened her womb. She conceived and bore a son and said, "God has taken away my reproach." And she called his name Joseph, saying, "May the LORD add to me another son!"
Genesis 30:22-24

"God, either You come into this room and meet me here, or I'll quit! Do you hear me God!? Either You come now, or I am done!" This was the violent cry coming from my mouth into the heavenlies as I choked back tears and allowed myself to be engulfed in the reality of my betrayal. To make matters worse, significantly worse, the betrayal was from God. It took all that I had to even sit in that room and ask for His Presence to come. It took every ounce of hope and energy that I had left.

About four months prior to that moment I was walking through my home only to hear the Lord say, "In two months, I am

1

removing your best friend and her family from within the church. They will step down from all leadership and leave the church indefinitely. If you are offended, know that your offense is with Me and when they tell you that I told them to leave, know that it was, in fact, my voice guiding them." They respectfully and honorably shared that God had told them to leave two months later, just as the Lord had spoken. My husband and I knew it was the Lord.

That was the hardest part. I knew it was the Lord. There was no reason that I could see for such a transition, yet, for ways that are higher than mine, God knew this was what needed to take place. I was distraught. I was more than distraught, I was, for the first time in my ministry experience, questioning my faith. Notice I did not say in my Christian walk, but rather, as a full-time pastor.There I sat, questioning who God was and what I believed. Pain has a very unique way of causing certain thoughts to surface that would, otherwise, never surface without that level of real and raw emotion.

My mind wanted to grab onto all the things that could have been wrong and settle on a reason for the departure that placed blame somewhere…just anywhere, other than on God. Yet, there I sat, knowing that God had done this. He warned me of it, and likewise, He told me my offense was with Him. He was absolutely right. As I sat there in that office chair, hot tears rolled down my face and anger ran through my heart. How could He do this to me? How could He make me endure this? I am not a newcomer to betrayal. I know it all too well. As does your pastor, his wife and your church leaders. It comes with the territory.

What about when the betrayal was God's idea? What do you

even do with such news? Some of you may be reading this thinking, "If God told me that, I would not be upset at all. I would trust that it was for the better, and I would know that good would come from it." If you have had that thought, that is absolutely incredible. Praise God. Today my thoughts are similar, but as the old cliche goes, "the first cut is the deepest." And it really is. This was the first ministry storm I had ever weathered, and as a young senior pastor's wife, I was quickly learning my foundation was a little shaky.

I WAS QUICKLY LEARNING MY FOUNDATION
WAS A LITTLE SHAKY.

I wept unwrapping the depth of rejection that I felt. I wept, considering the embarrassment that surely ensued as the news became public. Social media is vicious. I wept. If you paid attention to the time frame I gave you, this was two months after the initial departure. It took months before I could even sit down with God and talk about it. He is patient. As I wept, something began to happen that marked me forever.

Something that you read about and deeply hope would happen for you. Something you hear preached and long to experience. God's presence filled the room. His presence rushed into my office with such a weight, it felt like honey on my skin. In those next few hours, it felt like time and space came to a halt just for me. I communed with the Lord in a way that I had never communed with Him in my life. My eyes were opened to the realm of the Spirit, and I saw the angels ascending and

I saw the heavens open before my eyes. I was marked, forever. I was being positioned for what was to come.

I WAS BEING POSITIONED FOR WHAT WAS TO COME.

Night after night I went back into the office to meet with the Lord. I would sit and just wait. Like a faithful friend, He would show up again and again. He ministered to me, healed my heart and showed me great and hidden things. From the ashes of betrayal, came the greatest most impactful moments of my entire life.

On November 22, 2019 during one of my nightly visits with the Lord I was swept up into the Spirit, and I was shown what was to come. I saw the army of the Lord coming into my region with vigor and strength. I saw angels that had been sent on assignment to cause the sleeping church to wake up from her slumber. I saw that it looked to be great destruction, but the Lord was moving it in all. The Lord showed me that He would destroy our city with a tornado. He spoke of waking up the sleeping Church in our region, violently, as She had ignored His petitions. He told me that He was going to destroy the structure of what we called "church" and that it would all go to online platforms. He assured me that this was His doing, and He told me that once the tornado came through the city, we would know that it was time.

Revival

The Lord told me that revival would be poured out on our city, but only those who were awake and willing would welcome it. I shook as I recorded the word, just as He spoke it. What I am chronicling here is not all of the words that I was given that night, but it is what I feel led to share at this time. For the first time in my life, I felt the heart of God and His anger toward those who prostitute His Church. I felt the heat of His breath as He told me He wanted His Bride back.

On March 28, 2020, an EF3 tornado violently ripped through our town, destroying the center of our city. An estimated $300M dollars worth of damage was done. The eeriest part? It was just a normal day in Northeast Arkansas. There was no warning, very little appearance of a storm in the sky and the tornado came seemingly from nowhere. Minutes before the tornado dropped down out of the sky, my husband Zac and I were outside drawing with sidewalk chalk with our daughter. We came in just in time to see the news. Within minutes, the tornado was massive and deadly. Little did we know; it was headed directly for our home.

We ran into our guest bathroom with only some pillows and blankets, shaking. We were terrified. I will never forget Zac barely being able to whisper, "Jesus." It is all we could get out of our mouths. Our daughter, who was a very small toddler at the time, was screaming, and I was silent. I couldn't find the words. As the tornado approached our home it sounded like a freight train. The wind was roaring, and the sound was deafening. Our friends and church staff were frantically praying. This tornado came midday, and because it was in the middle of town, all the weather cameras had a perfect eye on the storm. They knew it was directly over our home.

Moments before the tornado touched our home, it had reached speeds of an EF4, but it suddenly changed directions. For what seemed like no reason at all, the tornado moved and began going right rather than straight, which is where our home was located. It leveled the homes at the end of our road, yet, we were left untouched. Again, we were being positioned for purpose. As the city came out of their homes to survey the damage that had been done, death seemed imminent. After all, there are very few EF3 tornadoes on record that did not take lives. There were 2x4 wooden planks sticking out of roofs, cars looked like smashed cans and major retailers were unrecognizable. Not a single death or major injury was reported.

IT WAS TIME FOR REVIVAL.

Undoubtedly, Rachel wept. God had opened the womb of her sister for her husband, Jacob, time and time again, yet Rachel remained barren. You may be familiar with this story. Jacob loved Rachel, and he had loved her from the moment he laid eyes on her. He worked for what the Bible says felt like a few short days, but was, in reality, seven long years for Rachel. He earned the right to marry her through completing the deal he had made with her father, Labon.

Yet, in a very shocking turn of events when Jacob asked for Rachel after completing his work, Labon deceitfully gave him Leah. It is fair to pause and ask how on earth a man could accidentally marry the wrong woman, much less her sister.

Nonetheless, the Bible tells us that is exactly what happened. Upon waking up from his marriage night, he found Leah laying next to him. He was, no doubt, justified in his furiousness. When he confronted Labon, Labon was deceitful, and told him that it wasn't right to give the younger before the older. He assured Jacob that he would give him Rachel also, in exchange for another seven years of labor of course.

The story unravels, as the sisters become rivals. Leah was hated and despised, yet blessed by God, while Rachel was loved and chosen, yet her womb remained closed. With the birth of each son, Leah said, "Now my husband will favor me." The Bible never tells us that Jacob found favor with Leah, but it does say that, with each son, Rachel hated her more. Rachel eventually says something rather interesting, which ties in our connecting points.

When Rachel saw that she bore Jacob no children, she envied her sister. She said to Jacob, "Give me children, or I shall die!"
- Genesis 30:1

It would be quite the journey before God opened her womb. We see that she gave her servants to Jacob as wives for the sake of birthing children on her behalf, but she had come to a breaking point of longing and desperation. She said, "Give me children, or I shall die." This reminds me of Hannah crying out in the temple for God to open her womb. When that finally happened, the man she birthed radically changed the world as we know it, and opened the prophetic womb, once again, for the people of God.

Samuel, the apostolic prophet, (as he is often referred to) caused sight and the word of the Lord to return to His people. (see 1 Samuel 1)

Rachel found herself, positioning for her purpose. Purpose is found in the places in which we experience the most resistance. It is found in the places where your heart's longings are so deep, words fail. "Give me children, or I shall die," Rachel said. "Come in here, or I will quit," I said. There is something very noteworthy about such moments. I would submit to you that these are kairos moments...God moments...fixed moments that God had appointed long before you even recognized the longing within. These are moments that God knew we would enter into, and so, they are moments that He was and is well-prepared to answer.

Then, God remembered Rachel, and God listened to her and opened her womb. She conceived and bore a son and said, "God has taken away my reproach." And she called his name Joseph, saying, "May the LORD add to me another son!" - Genesis 30:22-24

Then, God remembered Rachel, and He listened to her. She conceived Joseph. This is the man who would, one day, save the known world from a global famine. Yes, indeed, what may have just seemed like a sisterly rivalry was, in fact, a war for the physical salvation of the people of God. Today, we know and love the Twelve Tribes of Israel, yet they would not have survived to become the great nation of Israel, had it not been for the birth of Joseph. Rachel's longing for a son was much more than just grounds to prove herself as the superior wife. Her longing for a son was the longing that would, one day, save the sons of her rival, Leah.

Revival Breaks Out

While the world laid in wait for what would happen next, Zac, myself and our church staff cried out for revival. We were in the beginning stages of what was known as the COVID-19 Global Pandemic. Our city was recovering from the tornado, and we sought God. He told us that, regardless of what the rest of the world did, we were to meet again as a church on May 10th, 2020. He spoke plainly, and told us how we were to conduct our services. I want to make something very clear. We did as God instructed us. We did not look to the left or to the right, nor did we compare our church with what others were doing. We believe that every church body was doing what they felt led to do, and that is to be celebrated.

For us, God told us not to mandate masks, not to enforce social distancing, and He said for us to not fear. The first sermon my husband preached was on the leper who had to remain 6 feet from everyone around him and declare to everyone surrounding him that he was unclean, as he covered his ailments. Just as God said, revival poured out. There were only 25 of us in that first service, and all 25 of us were marked forever by what would soon become the very beginning of revival in Northeast Arkansas.

A literal, visible, cloud entered the room, and I saw grown men fly backward under the presence and power of God. Not a single person could stand under the weight of His glory as He visited us in strength, might and power. Very few around us understood what we were being asked to steward, but we knew. We had known for months, and we were being obedient, no matter the cost. Not a single COVID-19 outbreak has ever happened in our church. Not then, and not ever. What started with 25, soon became 50, and then, 75 overnight. Suddenly, we grew to 100. People have moved states and traveled from around the world to be in our weekly meetings. At the time of this writing (2022), we are a church of 100, with a massive impact. We have seen medically documented miracles, more deliverances than I can count, drug dealers saved and set on fire, as well as many, many souls added into the Kingdom of God and more testimonies than I can fit into this book.

Can Betrayal Birth?

Let's recall, though, how it all started. Remind yourself of how we began this journey together. "Come in here, or I will quit." Perhaps, recall what Rachel said, "Give me children or I will die." It did not start with a nice time of prayer and fasting. Those times are good and very powerful, but pain produces purpose in unprecedented ways, when it is submitted to God. Pain, betrayal, setback, accusation, persecution, fill in the blank; none of it goes without a cause. There is not a single thing in this life that you can or will experience that He won't use in and through you, if you just give it to Him.

Consider how Rachel's barrenness caused her to long for a son. Consider how my broken heart and the loss of a friend pushed me into realms of God that I didn't even know existed.

Comfort cannot produce. Comfort keeps you in conformity. Comfort sings a lullaby to your purpose until it is fast asleep. In adversity and opposition, purpose is birthed. In the place where you are pushed beyond yourself, that is where you find the Lord patiently waiting. I have often said that your greatest test is your testimony, and your largest mess is your message. My friend and brother in the faith, Apostle Charlie Howell says it like this, "The warfare is a prophecy." The pain is prophesying, but are you hearing the message? He who has ears, let him hear what the Spirit of the Living God says to His church.

The life circumstance, the warfare, the overwhelm; it is prophesying of a coming breakthrough. It is a path of preparation, a sign and a ground of testing. It is pointing to purpose, but do you have eyes to see where the sign is pointing? David would not have killed Goliath without, first, slaying the lion and the bear. Noah would not have survived the global flood without, first, surviving global rejection from all who knew him. Samuel would not have opened the prophetic womb of Israel without, first, having felt the pain of rebuking his own spiritual father. Atonement of sin came after Jesus' suffering on the cross.

And after you have suffered a little while, the God of all grace, who has called you to his eternal glory in Christ, will himself restore, confirm, strengthen, and establish you.
- Peter 5:10

Have you suffered a little while? If so, good! That means you are being prepared. If not, prepare yourself for what is to come.

None of us are exempt from the woes of this life; however, we do not mourn as those without hope. This life and all that comes with it can, and will, be used for the goodness and glory of God, if we are brave enough to choose to be positioned for purpose. Should we be a people who fear the world that we are left here to preach to? Should we, the people of God, doubt His saving power in the midst of trials? James 1:2-3 says, "Count it all joy, my brothers, when you meet trials of various kinds, for you know that the testing of your faith produces steadfastness."

Are You Steadfast?

In most charismatic and pentecostal circles, we shy away from discussing topics such as suffering, trials, hardships of various kinds, etc... It is as though we are subtly communicating that such things should never take place in the life of a believer. In this vein of thought, we leave the everyday believer susceptible to the fallacy that, if we serve God, nothing uncomfortable or hard will ever come our way. The latter is false. Not only will uncomfortable and hard things come our way, but they are actually promised. While God is not the doer of evil, evil will happen in this life as a result of the fallen world in which we live. In spite of the state in which the world operates, we can rest assured that when (not if) we endure such things, God WILL use them. The question that remains is this: "Will we let Him?"

Consider the story and life of Job. Many great afflictions came upon him, not because he was outside of God's will or because He had sinned against God, but rather, the opposite. Job endured such suffering because he was in the midst of God's will, and he placed himself right before Him. Again, remember what my brother, Apostle Charlie Howell, said, "The warfare is a prophecy." When we move beyond viewing the warfare and the hardships as the sure sign that we are in the wrong, and we enable ourselves to move into the realms and mysteries of the Spirit, we begin to see that the devil is only a pawn on a chess board; he has already been defeated at his own game.

THE WARFARE YOU'RE EXPERIENCING IS PROPHESYING

Nothing that this life throws at you can strip you of purpose, if you surrender it to God and allow His will to be made perfect through you. Remember, the warfare you're experiencing is prophesying. What is it saying?

Let's Pray

God, thank You that You cause purpose, even in my pain. Jesus, I know that You are not the initiator of pain, but You can and will use all things for the good of those who love You and are called according to your purposes. I am called according to Your purposes. I am chosen by You. I am loved by You. Father, I ask that You continue to show me my purpose in every area of my life. My life purpose, the purpose you have for my home and everything surrounding me. Help me to see Your purposes in everything that concerns me. I submit to You, the pain, suffering, torment, and shame. I submit it all to You. God, I don't want it, and if You can use it, then, by all means, use it, Lord. Use my life for Your glory. Cause all things to work together for my good, God. I love You. I honor You. I worship You! In Jesus name I pray, amen.

Memory Verse

"And we know that for those who love God all things work together for good, for those who are called according to his purpose." - Romans 8:28

2

Dreamers Dream

Now Joseph had a dream, and when he told it to his brothers they hated him even more.
Genesis 37:5

A lot took place in between Joseph's birth and when he started dreaming. He fled with his family from his grandfather Labon, and he saw his father reunite with his Uncle Esau. After this, he endured the family trauma of his half sister, Dinah, being captured, raped and treated like a prostitute, all while watching his brothers murder the male descendants of the family responsible for raping Dinah, who were already healing from the circumcision they deceived them into getting. Undoubtedly, Joseph was also marked forever by the name change and limp of his father after Jacob wrestled with God and became Israel. Arguably, though, the most impactful life event of all was, likely, when Joseph's mother, Rachel, died through the birthing of her second and last son, Benjamin. This was Joseph's only full-blooded brother.

**Now Israel loved Joseph more than any other of
his sons, because he was the son of his old age.
And he made him a robe of many colors.
Genesis 37:3**

Joseph was Jacob's favorite son. Today, we would likely never say that we have a favorite child. I assume some would, but it is safe to say, most would not. However, this idea of a favorite child would not have been uncommon for Joseph's day. The text says that Israel made Joseph a coat of many colors. This coat is significant and worthy of being examined before proceeding. Some scholars say this garment is one of the most, if not the most, famous garment ever to be made in human history. Modern pop culture has made entire movies about the coat, there are countless art pieces depicting what it could have looked like, and there is even a rose called "Joseph's Coat."

This coat was more than just a nice garment, though. It was significant, and it represented much more than just a coat. Most scholars believe that Joseph's coat of many colors represented Joseph receiving the birthright. In Genesis 49:22-26, when Israel is blessing his sons before he died, it furthers this assumption, as Israel blessed Joseph above all his other sons. This is important to note, because the birthright was very important in the history of God's people. The first born son was to receive the birthright, ensuring that he would receive a double portion of his father's inheritance, and he would become the leader of the family once the patriarch died. The son with the birthright also inherited the father's authority.

Clearly, Joseph was not the first son born to Israel, though, he was the first to be born to Israel from Rachel, who was Israel's favored wife. Still, this coat meant more than even just the birthright. It also represented favor, wealth and anointing. Anyone who would have seen Joseph in this coat would have known that he was a man of renown and someone to be respected. As clothes can represent many things in our modern society, it was also true for Joseph's culture. Clothing was important. Creating a coat of many colors was no easy or cheap feat in that time.

Notice that Joseph made the coat. This would have taken time...a lot of time. Dyes were not as readily accessible as they are today. There were no synthetic dyes or easy means of obtaining dyes. Dyes came from plants and animals. It is said that most fabric dyers would have used sea snails to create a purple garment, and it is estimated that it would take something of about 10,000 sea snails to dye even one clock the color, purple. Wearing a coat of many colors spoke loudly to all who laid eyes on the coat that this was an important man.

But when his brothers saw that their father
loved him more than all his brothers, they hated
him and could not speak peacefully to him.
- Genesis 37:4

His Rejection – Their Protection

Joseph's brothers could not even speak to him in a peaceful manner. True favor from God will cause you to be rejected, hated, slandered and misunderstood. Consider Psalms 5:12 that says, "For you bless the righteous, O LORD; you cover him with favor as with a shield." I love that verse, and I often quote it. One day, the Lord spoke to me about this. He said, "Natalie, have you ever considered why favor must cover you like a shield?" I said, "No, Lord." He spoke again and said, "Because my favor on your life will require my protection over your life." Just as pain has an odd way of pushing us into purpose, favor has an uncanny way of bringing out all the hidden junk from those around you.

Everyone loves you, and everything is fine, as long as you have or are as much or less than the people around you, but the moment that you have or become something more than what surrounds you, is the moment rejection ensues. This is for many reasons, mainly why hurt people, hurt people. A scarcity mindset lies by saying if you have something, it must mean that they never will because, certainly, there isn't enough favor to go around for everyone. That simply isn't true, though. Joseph was rejected and hated by the people who should have loved him because the favor of God rested on his life. If you are reading this right now, and you find yourself in a position similar to Joseph, know that you are in good company.

FAVOR HAS AN UNCANNY
WAY OF BRINGING OUT ALL THE
HIDDEN JUNK FROM THOSE
AROUND YOU

I can recall being hated and rejected many, many times in my life, long before I knew what my life would become. I faced fierce rejection. I have come to learn that, oftentimes, the enemy realizes who we are long before we do, and he doesn't wait around for us to find out before his plot against us begins. However, we see that their rejection of Joseph would, one day, become the protection their life desperately needed. As Jesus said on the cross, "forgive them Father for they know not what they do."

Now Joseph had a dream, and when he told it to his brothers they hated him even more. He said to them, "Hear this dream that I have dreamed: Behold, we were binding sheaves in the field, and behold, my sheaf arose and stood upright. And behold, your sheaves gathered around it and bowed down to my sheaf." His brothers said to him, "Are you indeed to reign over us? Or are you indeed to rule over us?" So they hated him even more for his dreams and for his words. Then he dreamed another dream and told it to his brothers and said, "Behold, I have dreamed another dream. Behold, the sun, the moon, and eleven stars were bowing down to me." But when he told it to his father and to his brothers, his father rebuked him and said to him, "What is this dream that you have dreamed? Shall I and your mother and your brothers indeed come to bow ourselves to the ground before you?" And his brothers were jealous of him, but his father kept the saying in mind. - Genesis 37:5-11

Family Anointing

Joseph was 17 years old when he had these dreams, according to Genesis 37:2. So, he was a very young man when the Lord began to speak to him about what was to come. God seals His plans and instructions for our lives within us while we sleep, (Job 33:15-16) and that is what was beginning at that time for Joseph. Little did he know, he was stepping into the family anointing. We often speak of demonic generational curses and heroic bloodline breakers, but very seldom, do we speak of generational blessings, generational gifts and family anointings. Why? We blatantly see them all throughout scripture, and for those with eyes to see; we also see them all throughout the church, today. Not only was Joseph the favored son, but now, he had also shown that he was the son who inherited his fathers anointing. You know the story. We call it "Jacob's Ladder."

Jacob left Beersheba and went toward Haran. And he came to a certain place and stayed there that night, because the sun had set. Taking one of the stones of the place, he put it under his head and lay down in that place to sleep. And he dreamed, and behold, there was a ladder set up on the earth, and the top of it reached to heaven. And behold, the angels of God were ascending and descending on it! And behold, the Lord stood above it and said, "I am the Lord, the God of Abraham your father and the God of Isaac. The land on which you lie I will give to you and to your offspring. Your offspring shall be like the dust of the earth, and you shall spread abroad to

the west and to the east and to the north and to the south, and in you and your offspring shall all the families of the earth be blessed. Behold, I am with you and will keep you wherever you go, and will bring you back to this land. For I will not leave you until I have done what I have promised you." Then Jacob awoke from his sleep and said, "Surely the Lord is in this place, and I did not know it." And he was afraid and said, "How awesome is this place! This is none other than the house of God, and this is the gate of heaven."
- Genesis 28:10-17

Joseph and Israel were dreamers of dreams. They were men who heard God in the night hour and interpreted what was spoken. Upon waking from this jaw-dropping dream, Israel (then Jacob) immediately interprets the dream, and says, "This is the gate of heaven." I would submit to you that is why Israel kept this saying in mind when Joseph shared his dreams with his brothers. Israel knew his son had heard from God, regardless of how he felt about what was said.

If you are holding this book in your hand, it is safe to assume that you have likely prayed to break generational curses and sins off of yourself and your bloodline, but have you ever considered the generational anointings and giftings on your bloodline as well? The Lord still remembers what He placed on your bloodline long before it was perverted or demonized. He has a plan and purpose for every bloodline on the earth today. He does not create without purpose. I hear the Lord speaking as I am writing this,

"Tell the people that I am unlocking the hidden anointings and mantles that rest on their families, for many who will read this are the keys to unlock the door for their bloodlines. Surely, I have visited them and brought to their remembrance all that I have spoken to their fathers. The time is now, and even coming, when the children will arise in what the fathers refused. Step into what I have placed upon your bloodline, and watch as the reconciling of nations takes place. For I have never forsaken you, nor will I leave the righteous begging for bread. I am the Lord your God, and in its time, I will hasten it."

"Announce arrivals, not moves." –Justin Allen

Joseph made the mistake many of us do when God speaks. He announced the dream to the people around him, prematurely. We can argue that Joseph was arrogant, as some scholars say, and we can assume that he wanted his brothers to know he would rule over them. Likewise, we could conclude that he was simply ignorant, and he did not mean harm by sharing the dream, but did so in immature zeal. Regardless which viewpoint you take, the principle remains the same; announcement incites war. A wise prophet recently told me, "announce arrivals not moves." Justin Allen, prophet and author of *Confessions of A Young Prophet.*

I was sharing with Justin about some recent warfare that we had experienced, and in the true nature of the prophet's office, he gently redirected my thoughts away from the attack and toward why I was in that particular position. After some close examination, I realized we had done just as Joseph had done. We announced the arrival before we arrived. Such an announcement incites war against the word, just as we see in Joseph's life. As you and I both know, God uses this for his good, and later on in Joseph's life, it all begins to make sense, but could this have been avoided, had Joseph not announced the dream?

My husband is pretty amazing when it comes to questions like this, always reasoning that what happened is what happened, and playing out different scenarios is pointless because we cannot go back to change the reality of what happened. To his point, I don't desire to get into the "what ifs", but I do desire to bring this principle to light in your life. Have you announced a word too soon or shared an idea prematurely? Many stop before they even get started because, in ignorance, they share the word with people around them for their critique. What God has asked of you can only be done by you. Taking a poll from the people around you will only incite confusion, at best, and war, at worst. Sometimes, such as was Joseph's case, it is better to keep the word, protect the word and watch it play out as God said. War against a premature utterance has killed more purpose than fear or failure ever will. Remember what my friend said, "Announce arrivals not moves."

When Sin Manifests

They said to one another, "Here comes this dreamer. Come now, let us kill him and throw him into one of the pits. Then we will say that a fierce animal has devoured him, and we will see what will become of his dreams."
- Genesis 37:19-20

The brotherly tension peeked at an all-time high when the

brothers decided to kill Joseph. They even mocked what Joseph told them, saying, "we will see what will come of his dreams." We see their anger grow intense so quickly, but if we back up a few chapters, we can see a more clear path as to why there was such rage in the hearts of Israel's other sons. Do you remember the story of Jacob and Esau? I briefly mentioned at the beginning of this chapter that Jacob and Esau had been reconciled since Joseph was born, but earlier in Genesis, we see a very troubled relationship between Jacob and Esau.

Jacob knew what it was like to not be the favorite of his father:

> **When the boys grew up, Esau was a skillful hunter, a man of the field, while Jacob was a quiet man, dwelling in tents. Isaac loved Esau because he ate of his game, but Rebekah loved Jacob.**
> **- Genesis 25:27-28**

Jacob also knew what it was like to be favored by God:

> **For the LORD has chosen Jacob for himself, Israel as his own possession.**
> **- Psalms 135:4**

Jacob cheated his brother, that he envied, out of his birthright for stew:

> **And Esau said to Jacob, "Let me eat some of that red stew, for I am exhausted!"**

(Therefore his name was called Edom.)   Jacob
said, "Sell me your birthright now."   Esau said,
"I am about to die; of what use is a birthright to
me?" Jacob said, "Swear to me now." So he
swore to him and sold his birthright to Jacob.
                    - Genesis 25:30-33

Then Jacob deceived his father, so he could steal the blessing of
his brother:

So he went in to his father and said, "My
father." And he said, "Here I am. Who are
you, my son?" 1Jacob said to his father, "I
am Esau, your firstborn. I have done as you
told me; now sit up and eat of my game, that
your soul may bless me."
                    - Genesis 27:18-19

When Esau learned that Jacob deceitfully stole his blessing, his
anger was so fierce, he sought to kill his brother:

Now Esau hated Jacob because of the
blessing with which his father had blessed
him, and Esau said to himself, "The days of
mourning for my father are approaching;
then I will kill my brother Jacob."
                    - Genesis 27:41

It Runs In The Family

We have spoken about generational blessings and anointings, yet we also see some other things being passed, generationally. This brotherly tension between Joseph and his brothers actually predates him. As my husband, Zac, always says, "Sin in the heart of the father will be made manifest in the hands of the son, if it is not repented of and dealt with." We also see this in Cain. It is often said that Cain is the first murderer in the Bible, but that isn't so. Adam was the first to commit murder in his heart.

The man said, The woman whom you gave to be with me, she gave me fruit of the tree, and I ate. - Genesis 3:2

Adam knew that God said if they ate of the fruit, they would die (Gen 2:17), yet Adam saw that Eve did not die after she ate the fruit. Adam stood with Eve, and he watched her eat of the forbidden fruit. Genesis 3:6 says, "she took off its fruit and ate, and she also gave some to her husband who was with her, and he ate". The Bible plainly says that Adam was with Eve when she ate of the fruit, and when he saw that she did not die, he ate too. When God came into the garden and asked Adam why they hid, his response was one of betrayal, and his heart was revealed. "The woman whom you gave to be with me, she gave me the fruit of the tree and I ate" (Genesis 3:12). Adam knew the wage of their sin was death, and he wanted to ensure that Eve was the one who received such punishment, instead of himself. When Cain murdered Able, it was a clear manifestion of the murder Adam committed in his heart against Eve. We could go on for many, many other scriptural references to solidify this point, but for time sake, we will move forward.

The rage and murder that the sons of Israel were filled with were generational issues that stemmed from their father, Jacob, and his brother, Esau. It is important to note this because sometimes what we are dealing with in ourselves and with those around us actually has much more to do with things that have already happened than with what is currently happening. Nonetheless, Joseph's brothers were ready to murder Joseph.

Uncover Him

So when Joseph came to his brothers, they stripped him of his robe, the robe of many colors that he wore. - Genesis 37:23

Joseph's brothers knew that before they could throw him into a pit, they first had to strip him of his robe. We spoke a lot about this robe prior to this moment for this very reason. They knew that they had to uncover Joseph before he could appear to be a slave or a beggar. By taking Joseph's robe they were stripping him of his identity, the favor that he walked in and the proof that would cause others to realize that this was an important man. The tactic was: cause Joseph to look like a slave or a beggar, so that he could become one.

The enemy will always try to uncover you, so he can attack you. In our modern context this will often look like getting you outside of spiritual covering and from being connected to a local church body. I love online ministry just as much as the next person, but I will make this one point unapologetically clear; your online mentor, coach, pastor, etc., does not excuse you from the command to be a part of a church body. The word blatantly tells us not to forsake the gathering (see Heb 10:25). I know you may not like that and you may even choose to put this book down because of that statement, but I have a commitment to preach the truth and not just what is popular.

Should you continue on, know that this is one of the most used tactics of the devil; to uncover you. Joseph's robe was a direct indicator that he was a loved son. It would have warded off the men who eventually drew him out of the pit and sold him. Covering wards off attacks that you are otherwise susceptible to. Covering communicates in the natural and in the spiritual. When the devil desires to really move in your life, the first thing he will do is try to uncover you. Don't allow this to take place. Guard your heart and your mind, show yourself approved by rightly dividing the word of God. Offense will come, but it is your glory to overlook offense (see Prov 19:11). I am not advocating for abuse, but accountability is not abuse and I love all of my readers enough to say that plainly.

Another form of uncovering that the enemy will use is the uncovering of your identity. He will try to strip you of your God given identity. We see this most often by his attempt to get believers to curse themselves. He cannot curse you, all curses were broken on the cross and hell has no power against you because you are covered in blood. What does have power against you though, is the power of the tongue and I would submit to you that your very own tongue has more power concerning your life than any other tongue. Recall Proverbs 18:12, "Death and life are in the power of the tongue, and those who love it will eat its fruits." There is power in your mouth, SO much power. The enemy knows that his power against you is unfruitful, yet your own God given power is very fruitful. The scripture clearly says you will eat its fruit. Why? Because the power in your tongue is bearing fruit whether you like it or not. Do not fall for this snare of stripping you of identity. If you have, renounce word curses against yourself through negative confession and be diligent to speak the word of God.

Come Out of the Pit

And they took him and threw him into a pit. The pit was empty; there was no water in it.
- Genesis 37:24

They threw Joseph into a pit. We don't know how big or deep the pit was, but we do know that there was no water in it. Undoubtedly, they had to have heard him screaming for help. After all, if his screams could not be heard, how would the Midianite traders know to draw him out of the pit? Reuben, the eldest brother, had convinced the younger ten to throw Joseph into a pit rather than kill him. The pit was the next best thing to murder. Let that sink in.

How often do we hear the phrase, "in the pits"? The Bible has a lot to say about pits, the bottomless pit often referred to as hell (see Rev 20), the blind fall into a pit (see Mat 15:14), a pit for the soul (see Psalms 35:7-8), the pit in which nations sink into (see Psalms 9:15), a pit dug for the wicked (see Psalms 94:13), a pit for the one who flees the report of disaster (see Isaiah 24:17-18), the pit dug for the prophet(s) by the enemy (see Jer 18:20-22), the lowest pit of dark places and depths (see Psalms 88:6), the deep pit of the mouth of an adulteress (see Prov 22:14), the deep pit of the harlot (see Prov 23:27), sheol; the recesses of the pit (see Isaiah 14:15; Job 33:18; Psalms 30:3) and many more. This is not an exhaustive list, but I think the point is made clear.

Pits were and are important places both physically, mentally, and spiritually. The pit that Joseph was thrown into was the next best thing to murder; it is worth repeating. When the various scribes of the Bible speak of the pit, they are referring to deep, dark, demonic places. After they stripped Joseph, they threw him into a pit. The devil knows he cannot take you out, for God's hand is upon you, yet if you are uncovered, he can and will throw you into a pit. We will continue on with who drew Joseph out of the pit and what happened next, but for now consider any pit that you may be in or have been in. It is time to come out of the pit.

Let's Pray

Oh Jesus, draw me out of the pit. Bring me out of any dark place that I may be residing in physically, mentally, or spiritually. Bring me out before You God, that I may worship at Your feet. Show me Lord the places where I have been uncovered or stripped of my identity. Restore to me Lord the days of my youth when the enemy encroached upon my life. Bring to my remembrance the many bloodline blessings that you have bestowed upon me. I plead the blood of Jesus over myself and over my bloodline. By the power and the authority of the name of Jesus Christ I break all generational curses from off myself and my bloodline right now in Jesus Christ name! I am a bloodline breaker. Sin does not run in my family any longer, but blessing abounds! In Jesus name, amen.

Make sure that you are following along in your Joseph; Positioned for Purpose Workbook. I have prayerfully created the workbook to go along with each chapter to ensure that your breakthrough is inevitable.

Memory Verse

O Lord, You have brought up my soul from Sheol; You have kept me alive, that I would not go down to the pit. (Psalms 30:3)

3

The Pit

Then Midianite traders passed by. And they [his brothers] drew Joseph up and lifted him out of the pit, and sold him to the Ishmaelites for twenty shekels of silver. They took Joseph to Egypt.
- Genesis 37:28, emphasis added

The warfare speaks of where you are going, not where you are. I began to face warfare almost seconds after accepting Christ. My life basically fell apart; thank God. Everyone (except my grandparents) in my life prior to my moment of salvation left my life within the week of my decision to follow Christ, every single one of them. Rightfully so, I mean, before Christ I was using drugs heavily and deeply involved in immorality. Upon accepting Christ and receiving massive deliverance, I had zero desire to participate in anything like that. I wanted to live holy before God. I was radically set free, forever.

Although prophets began prophesying over my life almost immediately after my salvation, I could not see how what they spoke would come to pass. That did not stop the enemy from launching attacks, right then, toward what was to come. I know I have already said it, but it bears witness again, "The warfare is a prophecy," (Apostle Charlie Howell). But can you hear what it is prophesying? I couldn't in those early years. No matter how many prophetic words were released over my life, and there have been many, I could not bridge the gap between the warfare that I faced and the reality I sat in. After all, I was just a young Christian fresh off of drugs; why was the enemy so fiercely and evidently after me?

If you find yourself in a state of preparation or warfare that seems unjustified for where you currently are, know that is a good sign. The warfare you face today has nothing to do with who you are today or the impact that you are making right now, but it does have everything to do with the assignment that is on your life. You face warfare based on the purpose, not on the current position. That means long before you step into all that God has called you to, you will walk through refining based on that end result. I pray that this brings language, clarity, and understanding to what you have faced, are facing, and will face in your positioning for purpose.

His Brothers Sold Him

In the midst of the warfare the enemy loves to use people close to you (especially family) to hurt you, in any way possible and the sheer irony is that what is happening in your life will directly affect theirs whether you ever see that in the natural sense like Joseph's family did or not. Make no mistake that the rejection you face for Christ will be at the hand of those who will

*Y*ou may not see it clearly now, but give it time and that reality will become abundantly clear. Let's read the full passage of how Joseph was sold into slavery and dive deep into its meanings for Joseph and for our lives today.

Now his brothers went to pasture their father's flock near Shechem. And Israel said to Joseph, "Are not your brothers pasturing the flock at Shechem? Come, I will send you to them." And he said to him, "Here I am." So he said to him, "Go now, see if it is well with your brothers and with the flock, and bring me word." So he sent him from the Valley Of Hebron, and he came to Shechem. And a man found him wandering in the fields. And the man asked him, "What are you seeking?". "I am seeking my brothers," he said. "Tell me, please, where they are pasturing the flock." And the man said, "They have gone away, for I heard them say, 'Let us go to Dothan.'" So Joseph went after his brothers and found them at Dothan.

They saw him from afar, and before he came near to them they conspired against him to kill him. They said to one another, "Here comes this dreamer. Come now, let us kill him and throw him into one of the pits. Then we will say that a fierce animal has devoured him, and we will see what will become of his dreams." But when Reuben heard it, he rescued him out of their hands, saying, "Let us not take his life." And

Reuben said to them, "Shed no blood; throw him
into this pit here in the wilderness, but do not lay
a hand on him"—that he might rescue him out of
their hand to restore him to his father. So when
Joseph came to his brothers, they stripped him
of his robe, the robe of many colors that he wore.
And they took him and threw him into a pit. The
pit was empty; there was no water in it.

Then they sat down to eat. And looking up they
saw a caravan of Ishmaelites coming from
Gilead, with their camels bearing gum, balm,
and myrrh, on their way to carry it down to
Egypt. Then Judah said to his brothers, "What
profit is it if we kill our brother and conceal his
blood? Come, let us sell him to the Ishmaelites,
and let not our hand be upon him, for he is our
brother, our own flesh." And his brothers
listened to him. Then Midianite traders passed
by. And they drew Joseph up and lifted him out
of the pit, and sold him to the Ishmaelites for
twenty shekels of silver. They took Joseph to
Egypt.

When Reuben returned to the pit and saw that
Joseph was not in the pit, he tore his clothes and
returned to his brothers and said, "The boy is
gone, and I, where shall I go?" -Genesis 37:12-30

There has been a lot of debate over this passage of scripture
over the years. Maybe you caught what some call "discrepancies"

The text says that brothers decided to sell him, yet it seems as though it says that Midinate traders drew him up and sold him to Ishmaelites who then sold him into Egypt. As I was studying and preparing to write this chapter, I kept wrestling with God over this as I read many viewpoints and scholarly debates over what took place. I kept asking God if it really mattered who actually sold him, after all is not the point that he was in fact sold? The more I wrestled with God and studied the text the more both the answer and God's need for me to see it became more clear. When Joseph is reunited with his brothers we see Joseph tell the story from his own account of who sold him.

"So Joseph said to his brothers, "Come near to me, please." And they came near. And he said, "I am your brother, Joseph, whom you sold into Egypt." - Genesis 45:4

Joseph says that his brothers are who sold him into Egypt, again the debate remains concerning why Reuben was so distraught when he saw that Joseph was gone as continuing in this viewpoint would mean that the brothers likewise deceived Reuben. The wind of the Spirit of God is upon this text as we study it and because of Joseph's personal account I believe the brother's of Joseph sold him. Let us remind ourselves of why they sold Joseph.

- It was the next best thing to murder.
- He was the favored son.
- He received the birthright.
- His dreams confirmed he held the birthright.
- He would one day rule over his brothers.

Herein lies a place for us to rest our thoughts for a moment, out of all the reasons scripture gives us for why Joseph was hated and sold, which of these was a fault of Joseph's? Yes, we can make the case that possibly Joseph was arrogant and told his brothers of his dreams to flaunt his clear favor, however, most scholars don't hold to that thought as much as we tend to lean toward his ignorance in just sharing a dream.

Then if Joseph had committed no clear wrong against his brothers, why were such awful things happening to him? Why was he so hated and shunned by the very men who were to love and protect him? Friends, the way that people treat you speaks to their own heart and never yours. If someone treats you with kindness and respect, that is because they themselves are kind and respectful. If someone treats you with malice and with hate, that is because they themselves are full of malice and hate. I desire to eradicate the idea that if hard, uncomfortable or even bad things happen to us that it must mean God is displeased.

This way of thinking is a slow poison that has crept into the church, one that we must address in its entirety and bring before the full counsel of God as found in His word. Joseph had committed no clear wrong, certainly there are no accusations or even suggestions of sin that we can see from the text. What is happening to him is clearly hatred, rage and anger from other men, yet God allows such behavior to take place. Is the cliche true, "bad things happen to good people?" I think not. I think that God's ways are higher than our ways and His thoughts are higher than our thoughts.

I think that there is a massive shift that we can have, one that breeds peace and a content heart when we surrender our need for control. We grapple with God and with the realities that we face and if we are honest, we desire to understand and control the situations we face and their outcomes. But what if we surrendered control? Even more painstakingly, what if we surrendered our desire to understand? Certainly this is not a simple mental choice we can make and never return to ask these questions again, yet what if our trust was truly in God and God alone? What if the moments that we are resisting most are the moments that are positioning us for purpose?

WHAT IF THE MOMENTS
WE ARE RESISTING ARE THE
MOMENTS THAT ARE POSITIONING
US FOR PURPOSE?

When we have such discussion it is without doubt that some immediately swing far on the pendulum of justice and say, "If God is good then how can such things happen?" While I have never read the book, I have been told by many that the book *The Problem with Pain* by C.S. Lewis is a fantastic text exploring such a subject. But I fear that our questioning of such matters has nothing to do with God or His word and it has everything to do with the depth of our need to understand.

The brain is such an interesting organ. I have studied it quite a bit as I suffered deeply from trauma, abuse and the like. I knew that if I could understand what my brain was doing by means of studying neuroscience, etc., that the likelihood of me healing from such moments and making lasting change was much more obtainable. I knew that if I could understand why something was happening, I would be more empowered to change it. Is this not our human existence in its whole? Understand why and it will all make sense, if it makes sense then I can move on, yet if it does not make sense my logic is left unserved and I am left in limbo, a state most people cannot stand to live in. This is also where blame placing and blame shifting comes heavily into play, as long as there is something to blame there is a why which means there is understanding.

In my studies of the brain I found this idea, or theory if you will, to be greatly backed by science and even discovered that this truly is the premise of modern therapy. While I have no desire to knock modern therapy or even the need to understand why, I certainly am bringing a new prowess to the church as it pertains to how we view what happens to us in our lives. Recall with me how we started this journey together. God told me what He was going to do, He did it but because I could place blame nowhere but on God alone it all but broke me. Ponder with me what would have happened if that betrayal had not happened. Would I have sought God with such fervor? Would I have come to the end of myself leaving me vulnerable to hear God in His true tone? Would I have received the word about the tornado or revival? Would our church have exploded in the midst of a pandemic had I not heard the Lord?

Our thinking is futile. At best it is limited and at worst, at times, it is demonic. The apostle Paul said in Romans 8:7 that our mind is hostile toward God unable to serve Him. That is why we are instructed to renew our mind and told that we have been given the mind of Christ. In our dyer state of needing understanding, are we not honestly putting on display our sheer lack of trust in God? That may sting, but let the Spirit of God bear witness to what is God. The anxiety, fear and overwhelm that we face is not because God is not good and allows evil to happen. No, in fact, we feel and face such things because our mind is set on the things of flesh and not the things of the Spirit. Please hear me, please. I do not desire to diminish even an ounce of pain that you have felt in your life, nor do I desire to take away from the very grim realities that I know many (including myself) have called their own.

OUR THINKING IS FUTILE.
AT BEST IT IS LIMITED AND AT
WORST, AT TIMES, IT
IS DEMONIC.

I buried my mother at 7. I was sexually abused at 5. I was told my father died when I was 6, yet found him alive when I was 18. I have been beaten, lived in a car, miscarried children, been left for dead and worked in places no woman should ever work. I know pain. Yet, I know purpose all the more. Many are astonished at my life. Comparing who I am today to who I was is like comparing a TD Jakes sermon to an episode of Cops. A little humor to lighten the mood, but in all honesty; I am a miracle. A miracle is writing this book with the desire to impart a miracle to you through the scribal anointing upon my life. The miracle of surrender. The miracle of fearless trust in God. The word of the Lord has come to me saying,

"They need to be told that they do not have to worry about such matters, that it is okay to move forward in praise with Me. For I will give them a garment of praise for the spirit of heaviness. In the world it is taught to them that if they do not

worry then they must not care, but the latter lacks wisdom. To not worry is to trust Me and to care is to give it to Me that I may work on their behalf. Can I not do more in six days than man can do with all of eternity? Can man create the sun or the moon? Can man cause a beast to come from the earth? So then, should not your trust lay in My hands? Here in this moment, give to me Your cares that I may sort them for you. Do not withhold from Me your pain nor hide your shame from My eyes, I Am who I Am and I Am healing you now in this very hour."

The Cover Up

Then they took Joseph's robe and slaughtered a goat and dipped the robe in the blood. And they sent the robe of many colors and brought it to their father and said,"This we have found; please identify whether it is your son's robe or not." And he identified it and said, "It is my son's robe. A fierce animal has devoured him. Joseph is without doubt torn to pieces." Then Jacob tore his garments and put sackcloth on his loins and mourned for his son many days. All his sons and all his daughters rose up to comfort him, but he refused to be comforted and said, "No, I shall go down to Sheol to my son, mourning." Thus his father wept for him.
- Genesis 37:31-35

The brothers went with haste to cover up what they had done. They knew their father would be distraught to learn that Joseph was "no more." It is interesting that they took the very robe that was an outward sign of favor and ruined it by dipping it into blood. There is so much prophetic symbolism here, but for the sake of not being too deep I will leave it for your own discussion with the Lord. Jacob, who was Israel, tore his garments and put a sackcloth on his loins. It was normal Jewish custom for Jew's to tear their clothing when they were in distress; it was an outward sign that they were mourning. The covering of his loins with sackcloth spoke to the harsh exposure he was experiencing as a father. The sackcloth would have had holes and not been a solid piece of fabric leaving Israel exposed to those around him. Likewise the cloth was a very harsh garment that was sometimes made of goat hair. Remember when we spoke about pits? One of the pits that we mentioned was the pit of sheol.

But you are brought down to Sheol, to the far reaches of the pit. - Isaiah 14:15

Joseph had been thrown into a pit by his brothers and so had Israel. He said, "I shall go down to Sheol with my son, mourning." Little did Israel know, Joseph did go down into "sheol", the pit, with great distress and mourning. All his sons and daughters rose to comfort him, yet he could not be consoled. Isn't that just like the devil? To try to comfort you from the very onslaught he has released against you. When I was a teenager my laptop was stolen, I remember being so upset that it was stolen because it had all the photos of a relationship that, at the time, was meaningful to me. A friend consoled me as I was so upset over the loss of my laptop. Weeks later I would find out that the very friend who consoled me was the friend who stole my laptop. When my grandparents went to her home to receive it back from her parents, they had destroyed it in the backyard fearing that we would press criminal charges against the girl. I would not have done that, but have you ever had something like that happen to you?

Hopefully you have not, but if you have you know the sting. A stolen laptop is no comparison against the perceived death of a son, but the tactic remains the same. They consoled their father while he mourned the "death" of a son that they had sold off to Egypt. It makes you wonder what went through their minds, maybe there was remorse or maybe they thought this was their chance for someone else to be the favorite. Either way, Israel went down to sheol to mourn.

Let's Pray

Father, Help me to forgive those who have wronged me and expose the times when the devil has tried to console me while I mourned the work he had caused. Bring me out of the pit oh God and forget me not in Sheol. Bring me into gladness and help me oh God to live upright before You. Empower me to forgive for I cannot do this great work without Your hand upon my life. Help me surrender my need for constant understanding and momentary control. I lean into Your understanding, trusting that it is far greater than mine. I give You my fearless trust that You may use all things in my life to work together for Your good. In Jesus name, Amen.

Memory Verse

Trust in the LORD with all your heart, and do not lean on your own understanding. (Proverbs 3:5)

4

The Preparation

Meanwhile the Midianites had sold him in Egypt to Potiphar, an officer of Pharaoh, the captain of the guard.
Genesis 37:36

More often than not, the preparation is harder than what you are actually being prepared for. Consider professional athletic teams as an example; they train in season and out of season. They train for hours on end when there are no lights, no cameras, and no opponent to face, to stand in the game for a fraction of the time they spent preparing for it. In 2008 when Michael Phelps was swimming in the Beijieng olympics his goggles filled with water causing him to swim most of the race essentially blind. When they interviewed Michael about this he simply explained that he had trained in perfect circumstances and imperfect circumstances, the imperfect being with his goggles filled with water. Even without sight, he won the gold medal and set a record for the most gold medals ever won by one person in the same olympic game.

You may have guessed that I am not a sports fanatic, however the principle stands that if you are well prepared for what you are stepping into, doing the actual task will be the easiest part. Preparation takes mental fortitude, foresight, and adaptability. Many are in the season of preparation though they do not understand how or even why. Preparation will make or break you. Consider Noah who built the Ark for 75 years, he had been rejected by the known world; preparing him for the day when he had to figure things out without the known world. David killed the lion and the bear before he faced and slayed Goliath. We see this same scenario playing out in the life of Joseph as he enters the house of Potiphar in preparation for what was to come with Pharaoh.

While Israel mourned, Joseph was sold to Potiphar, an officer of Pharaoh, the captain of the guard. Potiphar is an interesting study as his name means "the one who Ra (the sun god) gave". He was a military official, but the Hebrew term used to describe his military allegiance was often used to describe eunuchs. We know that Potiphar was not a eunuch as he had a wife and children (see Gen 39; 41:45), but the use of the word does seem to indicate that he was a very dedicated man to Pharaoh. His second title "captain of the guard" can be directly translated as "chief of the slaughterers." If we could leave literary discretion behind for a moment and clearly say it, he was a bad dude. Certainly not a man that you would want to cross or have a bad run in with.[1]

---

[1] Emil G. Hirsch and J. F. McLaughlin. "Potiphar or Poti-ferah," Jewish Encyclopedia, 1906, https://www.Jewishencyclopedia.com/articles/12316-potiphar. Accessed 22 Nov, 2022..

We also know that Potiphar was a priest of On (see Gen 41:45), also known as Heliopolis. Heliopolis is one of the most ancient Egyptian cities and it was also considered the "seat" of the sun god, Ra.[2] All of this is important to note, because Joseph was not entering into a place with people of importance, but rather he was being positioned with a family that was of noble regard to the Egyptians. It is also interesting to note the spiritual implications of what was taking place in Potiphar's life as a priest of a false deity. Undoubtedly the spiritual climate was intense. Egypt was known for its many pagan gods and idolatry worship. Joseph was not only learning how to live amongst Egyptians, he was also learning the culture of Egyptian power and the ins and outs of their spiritual culture.[3]

FIGHTING AN ENEMY THAT YOU KNOW AND HAVE AN UNDERSTANDING OF IS CERTAINLY EASIER THAN FIGHTING SOMETHING COMPLETELY UNKNOWN.

We know that Joseph remained faithful to God, but I would submit to you that God allowed Joseph to see the dark arts that took place behind closed doors as a part of his preparation. Fighting an enemy that you know and have an understanding of is certainly easier than fighting something completely unknown. Likewise, I would submit to you that this is why the scripture explains so much to us about the powers of darkness and how they work, so that we will not fear and will have understanding when we yield the authority given to us by Christ against the enemy.

---

2 Ibid.
3 Gary Rendsburg. "YHWH's War Against the Egyptian Sun-God Ra," The Torah, 2022, https://www.thetorah.com/article/yhwhs-war-against-the-egyptian-sun-god-ra.

Afterall, fear is worship. I will never forget the first time that I was slain by the power of the Holy Spirit on May 9th, 2020. When I hit the ground the Lord spoke these words to me, "Natalie, fear is worship. You cannot fear the devil lest you worship him. Fear and worship are reserved for Me and Me alone." I got up from that encounter changed. I had an understanding of warfare that I had not understood before; fearing warfare is worshiping it. Fearing the demonic is worshiping it. Second Timothy 1:7 says, "For God gave us a spirit not of fear but of power and love and self-control." That scripture suddenly made a lot more sense to me. I was not given a spirit of fear! And neither was Joseph.

The LORD was with Joseph, and he became a successful man, and he was in the house of his Egyptian master. His master saw that the LORD was with him and that the LORD caused all that he did to succeed in his hands. - Genesis 39:2-3

Even in slavery Joseph became a successful man. Let me pause and preach through this book for a moment. If you are worried your blessing can't find you in your season of preparation, if you have bought the lie that success comes after you have completed the process, if you have fully submitted to the idea that the preparation is hard, allow the word of God to set you free today! Joseph was blessed in slavery. God was with him in slavery. In fact, Joseph was so blessed that the man who was enslaving him recognized that God was with him and for him.

It may feel like people are watching your season of trial closely and it may seem as though they have the upper hand, but you make no mistake; those who have their eyes on you in your season of preparation see GOD! Whether they ever admit it or not, they see God moving in your life. They see His hand upon you. That is why they are shaken that you keep going. That is why it bothers them that you can keep your head up in the middle of all that you have walked through, they know God is with you and for you and they cannot be against you.

I prophesy that in this season of preparation your blessing is going to hunt you down. I prophesy that your eyes are being opened even now to the reality that you are blessed in this season and that God deems you successful even in the midst of what might feel like a stalled out wasted season. Breath and fire is coming onto your dry bones even now in Jesus name. If that word hit your spirit, pause from reading and worship the Lord. Cry aloud to Him. Get on your knees and thank Him that your success is measured by heaven and never by man. Even in what looks like slavery to man, God calls you successful. Success does not come from what you do, but who you are! God is with you!

So Joseph found favor in his sight and attended him, and he made him overseer of his house and put him in charge of all that he had.
- Genesis 39:4

Potiphar made him overseer and put him in charge of all that he had. A slave, in charge of all that Potiphar has. Now, we know the end of the story from the beginning, though Joseph did not as he lived this out. Does this not sound familiar?

You shall be over my house, and all my people shall order themselves as you command. Only as regards the throne will I be greater than you." And Pharaoh said to Joseph, "See, I have set you over all the land of Egypt." - Genesis 41:40-41

Thus he set him over all the land of Egypt.
- Genesis 41:43

God was positioning Joseph in the house of Potiphar to reign well as the overseer of Egypt under Pharaoh. Pharaoh put Joseph in charge of all the land, over all his house and over all his people. Likewise, Potiphar put Joseph in charge of all that he had. Joseph was being prepared on a smaller scale for what he would one day steward on a global scale.

Are you faithful with the little that God is giving you to steward right now? Right now it may seem small, you may only have the ability to do a little, but are you faithful with the right now or are you always waiting for the "when it finally happens?" Friend, you will never steward Pharaoh's house well if you do not first steward Potiphar's house well. Joseph entered Potiphar's house as a slave and served well. Joseph entered Pharaoh's house as a ruler and reigned well. The purpose does not come without the preparation. What good Father would send their children out totally unprepared? God prepares us for where He is taking us and usually long before we even know we are being prepared for what we are being prepared for.

The Bible gives us zero indication that Joseph knew he was

being prepared to steward something great. Sure his dreams gave indication that his brothers would bow down, but isn't it most likely that Joseph felt that was an indication of his birthright? I would assume that Joseph felt there was no way that those dreams would take place now. Maybe he did, the text does not say, but it is certain that when Joseph was in the middle of it all he did not know he was being prepared for something.

Are you in the middle of your story right now? Do you recall the big prophetic word that was spoken over your life long ago, but now it seems there is just no way that can take place? The middle is often the hardest place to be in. The beginning is set ablaze by the call, the zeal of the purpose and the fresh fire on the word God has spoken. The end is the fulfillment and a new set of reality settles as we wrestle with the fulfillment being complete. That is a whole other book, honestly. Yet in the middle, we are so far from the beginning the fire has faded. We don't know how far we are from the end and the waiting can be, if we are honest, just brutal. The middle is where you are being prepared, if you find yourself sitting in a season that seems as though it has absolutely nothing to do with what God originally said yet you are serving Him, honoring Him with your life and submitting to Him in all your ways; you are in a great place my friend.

Look around and begin to take notice of what you are doing right now. Pay attention to the insight you are gaining from this season and the skills that you are learning. My husband has a bachelor's degree in Finance. In his third year of college, he got radically saved and surrendered to ministry not long after. He desperately wanted to quit college as he saw no real reason for the degree anymore. When he initially enrolled in college he was going to learn how to run a business, so he could take over his fathers used car dealership.

With the new fire and zeal of his new found purpose of being a pastor and church planter, he just did not see the point of finishing his business degree. Some pastor friend's encouraged him to finish, so that he could go to seminary which would require a bachelor's degree to be accepted. Reluctantly, he finished his business degree under the guise of "I have to do this to go to seminary." He did go to seminary and eventually, after we married, we planted a church (the one I've told you so much about already). Not only did the business degree, that be gained in the middle when it seemed pointless and like it had nothing to do with his purpose, come in clutch time and time again, it has also set our church up for massive sustainability. He uses his business degree every single week when looking at the major church budget that we are responsible for stewarding well. If he had left college and not received that training, we would have to rely on a CPA to help guide our financial decisions for the church. In the middle it seemed like it was pointless, yet God was using it to sustain Zac's purpose 12 years later.

From the time that he made him overseer in his house and over all that he had, the LORD blessed the Egyptians house for Joseph's sake; the blessing of the LORD was on all that he had, in house and field. So he left all that he had in Joseph's charge, and because of him he had no concern about anything but the food he ate.

- Genesis 39:5-6

Potiphar's house was blessed because Joseph was there. There is so much that can and should be said about this. God blessed a demonic priest's house, because one of his servants was a servant of God. Think about that for a moment, consider the magnitude of that. When God's favor is on your life, it will spill over into every area around you including to those connected to you in any way regardless of who they worship. There are two thoughts that I would like to share concerning this.

WHEN GOD'S FAVOR IS
ON YOUR LIFE, IT WILL SPILL
OVER INTO EVERY AREA
AROUND YOU.

The first thought is, sometimes your blessing is because of who you are connected to. This works both ways. There can be favor on your life that spills over onto others and there can be favor on others that spills onto you. An example I like to share concerning this is Samuel and the Sons of the Prophets. When Saul sent his servants to Samuel each of these servants began to prophesy just from being in the presence of Samuel and the other prophets. Even Saul began to prophesy and became like another man when he got in their presence (See 1 Samuel 19). The corporate anointing for prophecy was so strong on Samuel and the company of prophets that he was raising up, that it spilled over onto others even before the baptism of the Holy Spirit was poured out. I have seen instances where people have come into a gathering, begun to operate in something they've never operated in or in a new measure and not even realize it is because of the corporate anointing on the house or gathering. It is important to recognize what is being blessed because God is blessing you and what is being blessed because of who God is blessing you through. Community is an essential part of this Christian walk. If you do not have that, you need to find it and fast!

The second thought I want to share here is that when the favor of God is on you everyone around you will be blessed by it. I have a friend who is very favored by the Lord, it is obvious the evidence is all over his life. When he started working in his family business the business was successful, but since he started he has single handedly grown the business by millions and millions of dollars. His parents directly benefit from the favor that is on his life, it has made them multi millionaires. Whether they ever see that it is God's favor on their son or not, it is. When I started working for a local staffing agency in year one of our church plant, I immediately skyrocketed the sales. In just one year of being there I had, single handedly, grown the revenue in the business by over $1M. When God's favor is on your life, it overflows.

We discussed so much in this chapter that I know will directly apply to your life and current season. I can't wait to hear the testimonies from this chapter alone.

Let's Pray

Father, thank you that you are preparing me even when I don't realize it. Thank you that you are positioning me for purpose and ensuring that I am well equipped to do and be all that you are asking of me. I praise Your Holy name, Lord Jesus. You truly have caused what the enemy meant for evil and turned it for my good. In Jesus name, amen.

Memory Verse

Prepare your work outside; get everything ready for yourself in the field, and after that build your house. (Proverbs 24:27)

5

Accusations

**Blessed are you when others revile you and persecute you and
utter all kinds of evil against you falsely on my account.
Matthew 5:11**

"Get back to the simple gospel and stop making it [your
worship] such a theatrical show!" The words stung as I read them
off the screen, isn't it more interesting that a certain boldness
takes hold of people when they are behind an iPhone screen yet
that boldness fails to find them when they are standing with you
face to face. Afterall, I had been standing in this person's home
not long before they sent this message and they acted like
everything was fine. Clearly, it was not fine. That, however, is
honestly some of the lighter accusations I've received over the
years. Accusations are the enemy's ploy to assassinate.

John 10:10 says, "The thief comes only to steal and kill and
destroy. I came that they may have life and have it abundantly."

False accusations are bullets crafted by the enemy and fired by the mouth of anyone who will surrender themselves as a weapon of war, Christians included. In fact, most often accusations come from those who claim to be followers of Jesus. Sure, there are times when unbelievers yield accusations and such our way, but have you ever noticed that it is honestly very hard to get offended at a total unbeliever? They do not know, they are wandering like a sheep without a shepherd. After all, do we not expect lost people to act like lost people? We have abundant grace for them in their journey of trying to understand the truth.

It really is when a brother or sister acts like a lost person in their pursuit of character assassination that is mind blowing. It almost catches us off guard and even worse, if we let it, we begin to question if they are right about us. That is when you know the enemy is at work. See, the Bible gives us clear instruction for how we are to handle such matters amongst Christians in Matthew 18.

"If your brother sins against you, go and tell him his fault, between you and him alone. If he listens to you, you have gained your brother. But if he does not listen, take one or two others along with you, that every charge may be established by the evidence of two or three witnesses. If he refuses to listen to them, tell it to the church. And if he refuses to listen even to the church, let him be to you as a Gentile and a tax collector.
- Matthew 18:15-17

We are to go to the person one on one, then two on one, then before the church and if they refuse to hear us then we should treat them as a Gentile or a tax collector. Here is the irony in this though, Gentiles and tax collectors in this passage are representing those outside God's people and sinners meaning we should try to win them to the Lord. How much more do we show grace to the lost as we just spoke about? When brothers and sisters in Christ bring accusations against you without following this protocol, know for certain that satan is behind the work. God does not desire that we live in contention with one another or in divisions. He desires that we live in unity and peace, even if we cannot agree on the matter. Paul and Barnabas split ways after a dispute, yet they did so peaceably (see Acts 15:36-41).

ALLOW CONVICTION TO HAVE ITS FULL WORK AND COMMAND CONDEMNATION TO GO

This works both ways, I am sure you are sitting here reading this thinking of many times when this has happened to you. If you have served God for any amount of time or are making a real impact for Him, these things will happen. Period. It is not if, it is when. Yet, I want to lovingly challenge you and ask, when have you surrendered yourself to be a weapon that satan could use against someone else? We are human. We are imperfect and make mistakes. Forgive those who have treated you this way, but likewise repent if you have treated others this way. Whether that looks like prayer or a phone call, you pray and ask the Lord. Remember condemnation says, "I can never change, I am terrible." Conviction says, "I am empowered by God to live according to the standard He has set for me." Allow conviction to have its full work and command condemnation, which is fear, to go in Jesus name.

Joseph is Accused

I felt it necessary to discuss accusations in a more modern context and in a very applicational way to open the chapter, because let's face it; it is going to happen and we need to have biblical understanding for how to move past it. Remember that the only accusation that will ever truly bother you is the one you fear is right, either because you loved and trusted the person who said it and their opinion mattered to you or because you are actually insecure about that area of your life. The enemy loves to prey on our insecurities. Either way, fearing that they are right is the real reason such things bother you. If they are right, repent before God and be reconciled; whatever that looks like for that relationship. If they are not right, forgive them and move on.

Joseph found himself in a very interesting situation when Potiphar's wife accused him of raping her before Potiphar and the men who worked for him. Character assassination at its finest. There is so much that we can learn about how the enemy uses accusations from this portion of Joseph's story.

Now Joseph was handsome in form and appearance. And after a time his master's wife cast her eyes on Joseph and said, "Lie with me." But he refused and said to his master's wife, "Behold, because of me my master has no concern about anything in the house, and he has put everything that he has in my charge. He is not greater in this house than I am, nor has he kept back anything from me except you, because you are his wife. How then can I do this great

**wickedness and sin against God?" And as she
spoke to Joseph day after day, he would not
listen to her, to lie beside her or to be with her.
- Genesis 39:6-10**

She cast her eyes on Joseph. She looked and she saw
something that she wanted; in this case it was sex, but before she
actually tried to seduce him she looked at him. Pay attention to
those who are always "looking" into your life, the enemy can
work in subtleties and outright requests. I have noticed over my
years in ministry there are certain women who will look at my
life, especially the people close to me and determine that they
desire that in my life. They desire to be the person I call when I
need help or they desire my attention, affirmation, etc. It is one
thing to need ministry, it is a whole other thing to determine you
want to be an important part of someone's life and start trying to
make that happen on your own.

After looking at him for a while, she made her request known
to him and said, "lie with me." She attempted to seduce him into
sexual immorality. This is an obvious indicator that this is a
jezebelic spirit. Before full out character assassinsation there is
usually a subtle or in this case, not so subtle seduction that
happens. There is usually some sort of request that is made, "be
closer to me" or "I wish we could spend more time together." It is
important to note that both in a sexual sense and a non sexual
sense seduction usually begins with the request being made
known. This is why it is important that you lean not on your own
understanding, but rather on the word and the discernment that
God has given you. Whether the request is subtle or overt like
with Joseph, you have to trust the discernment that God is giving
you. He is protecting you.

Joseph fiercely answers her and refuses the invitation. He explained that his master has been good to him and he would not repay good with evil and he also says he will not commit the sin against God. Yet, she persisted day after day. Once the request is made known and it is met with rejection, there is a wearing out process the enemy will try to use. It is like when your child asks you for candy, some days you are strong and say no, but after so long of being worn down you give in. Just because people in your life are consistent does not mean that they are there for the right reasons. I have had people in my life for years and years before their true motive finally fully surfaced. Trust your initial discernment. The world calls this the "first impression." While I don't subscribe to first impressions, I do know that the first thing that I discern is always the right thing and even if it takes years; it always surfaces. Stop letting your heart talk you out of what your spirit already knows.

But one day, when he went into the house to do his work and none of the men of the house were there in the house, she caught him by his garment, saying, "Lie with me." But he left his garment in her hand and fled and got out of the house. And as soon as she saw that he had left his garment in her hand and had fled out of the house, she called to the men of her household and said to them, "See, he has brought among us a Hebrew to laugh at us. He came in to me, to lie with me, and I cried out with a loud voice. And as soon as he heard that I lifted up my voice and cried out, he left his garment beside me and fled and got out of the house." Then she laid up his garment by her until his master came home, and

she told him the same story, saying, "The Hebrew servant, whom you have brought among us, came in to me to laugh at me. But as soon as I lifted up my voice and cried, he left his garment beside me and fled out of the house."
- Genesis 39:11-18

Notice that she makes her move when they are alone, there are no witnesses, when Joseph is vulnerable or weakened as he is alone. The enemy attacks when you are alone, that is why community is so important. Day after day she harassed him, but when they were alone she attacked him. She grabbed him by the garment, but he fled. Once she saw that his garment was in her hand, she knew she now had "evidence" so she could make her case. The interesting thing about when the enemy comes at you like this is he will use rejection and embarrassment to drive the person he is moving through.

Potiphar's wife likely felt rejected and embarrassed that she was begging a man to have sex with her, literally throwing herself on him, yet she was told no again and again and again. Rejection will drive unhealed people to do some pretty wild things. The Bible does not tell us that she had ever done this to another man, but it makes you wonder if the other men who worked for Potiphar had laid with her. It is possible she was not accustomed to being told no. That is of course only speculation, but an interesting one for sure.

Once she had what she considered evidence, the character assassination was in full force. Jezebel fueled with rejection will collect evidence along the way. It will hold on to any "article" that it can get its hands on. For Joseph it was his actual clothes.

For us it may be conversations, moments, text messages, screenshots of misinterpreted Facebook posts and the list goes on. Nonetheless, there will be a compiling of evidence, because when Jezebel finally fully attempts to assassinate your character, know that she has been preparing to do that since the first time you rejected the invitation. Erie isn't it? To think back to moments when you were around someone who claimed to love you, but inwardly they were collecting their evidence. First Corinthians 13:5 says this about love, "It does not dishonor others, it is not self-seeking, it is not easily angered, it keeps no record of wrongs." So, know that when someone has compiled their evidence and they are attempting to assassinate your character, they are not being driven by God, but by demons or their own wicked flesh. Love does not operate in records of wrong.

Jezebel Will Attack the People Around You Too

Notice that when she ran outside to tell the other men, she started by blaming her husband. She said, "see he has brought among us a Hebrew to laugh at us." Her rejection was so overt that now she was blaming both Joseph and Potiphar. This is especially interesting because the enemy loves to attack both you and anyone who could protect you. He does this to try and gain influence and control over those it desires to persuade. He attempts to build a firm case, so no one will question what he is doing. If the scheme is questioned, the defensive nature will speak all for itself. Love does not fear being questioned, but seeks all to know the truth. The devil fears questioning always and uses intimidation through a defensive attitude to cause the one with questions to back down.

Blame shifting is a practice that the devil loves to operate in. It will always call the person it is attacking the very thing that it is. Potiphar's wife was sexually harassing Joseph, so she cried out that Joseph was sexually harassing her. I like to say it like this, the one screaming that everyone else is a Jezebel is the Jezebel. This is a tactic that this spirit uses almost indefinitely.

BLAME SHIFTING IS A PRACTICE THE DEVIL LOVES TO OPERATE IN.

As we spoke about earlier, there is a clear distinction between coming to someone in love and concern and assassinating someone's character. When you see people screaming aloud trying to assassinate people in hopes to change the perspective and opinions of other people toward that person, all the accusations they bring against the other persons are usually the very thing they themselves are doing/operating in. They are projecting.

Recently I was on a one on one call for my business. I was interviewing a young woman to see if she would be a good fit for my coaching program. Throughout the call she explained that she is a minister, but she does not believe what she says as she ministers. She went on to say that she doubted what she said so much that she also doubted other ministers who ministered to her. At the end of the call I told her I felt my program would benefit her and offered her the opportunity to enroll in working with me. Her response was almost shocking, she explained that there was no way I could help her, because I help so many people through books, social media, our church, in my coaching program, etc.

She went on and on about how there is simply no way I could help so many people and be genuine. See the connection there? She accused me of the very thing she was doing; not being genuine in helping people. I am not asserting this woman had a demon, but I am certainly asserting that most often when people bring accusations against you they are really just telling what they themselves are dealing with by projecting it on to you.

The Truth Does Not Care What it Looks Like

Potiphar's wife lied and said Joseph left his garment beside her when she lifted up her voice and cried aloud. The truth was that she caught him by his garment and said, "lie with me" and Joseph fled, running out of the house. Things are not always what they seem, let this be a perfect example of that for you. Just because it may appear as though someone has solid evidence to back up what they are saying, you better have the Spirit of God to direct and guide your discernment on matters.

Never take someone's silence in defending themselves to be the confirmation that the accusers are right; in fact, allow that to scream loudly that the truth speaks for itself. The text never tells us that Joseph defended himself or even that he was concerned that he left his garment in her hand. The truth does not care what it looks like. There is one side to every story and that is the truth. The truth of a matter does not have to be defended, it stands the test of time while the accusations of the enemy will be exposed and put to open shame; no matter how long it takes. Know that you do not have to defend the truth of a matter, because truth defends itself.

**The LORD will fight for you, and you have only
to be silent." - Exodus 14:14**

**Beloved, never avenge yourselves, but leave it to
the wrath of God, for it is written, "Vengeance is
mine, I will repay, says the Lord."
- Romans 12:19**

Joseph was punished for this crime, although he did not commit it. Yet, as we will read in the next chapter, God was with him all the more and even in what felt like his accuser having an upper hand on him; God was still positioning him for purpose. God wastes nothing. He is so good. No matter where you sit at the end of this chapter, whether you are someone who has assassinated someone's character only to now realize that was not the way to handle it or if you have had someone wrongfully accuse you and damage your character in the eyes of others; know that God can and will use all things for the good of those who love Him.

If you are like Potiphar's wife and you have built cases against others, because deep down you felt rejected and embarrassed; repent. Cry out to the Lord and He will meet you there. He loves you and He will forgive. Ask the Lord if action is required on your part after repentance, such as an apology. He is just and will direct your steps.

If you are like Joseph and you have had fierce accusations come against you in an attempt to assassinate your character, know that no matter how much it may appear like the enemy won that battle; he didn't. God will take the very thing that the enemy sent against you and use it against the enemy. You need only to be silent and let the Lord fight for you. It is that fearless trust that we discussed at the beginning. Don't fight it. Don't rally people onto your side. Just know that you are blessed because of it. I know it hurts, I know it hurts deeply, but cry out to the Lord and He will comfort you.

Beloved, do not be surprised at the fiery trial when it comes upon you to test you, as though something strange were happening to you. But rejoice insofar as you share Christ's sufferings, that you may also rejoice and be glad when his glory is revealed. If you are insulted for the name of Christ, you are blessed, because the Spirit of glory and of God rests upon you.
- 1 Peter 4:12-14

At what hand did Christ suffer? Did He suffer at the hand of the world or at the hand of the church? Friend, He suffered at the hand of His own people, those who knew His word inside and out, taught in His temples and proclaimed to know God yet did not recognize Him when He stood face to face with them. Therefore, when you suffer at the hand of those who claim to know God, know that you are sharing in Christ's sufferings. Forgive as you have been forgiven. Extend mercy and repay a curse for a blessing. Above all things, love one another and keep your heart pure before God. "Perfect love casts out fear" (1 John 4:18). Do not fear what the enemy has attempted to do in your life, but rather ask God to perfect His love within you. Stand firm. God is with you.

Let's Pray

Father, be with me and show me your mighty hand working in my life even now oh Lord. I praise you for taking all things and using them for your good. You cause what was darkness to become light by exposing it to your light. You take what was once used against me and turn it into a testimony to bring others into Your Kingdom. I love you God for who is like You in all the earth? By what name can man be saved except by the name of Jesus Christ! You are great. Your mercies endure forever and You are a joy from age to age. Cause Your glory to arise and shine upon me, Lord! Cause every tongue that rises against me to be found false. Bring me into an even deeper revelation of how You truly are using all things to work together for Your plan. Show me Lord how you take what was meant for evil and use it for good. Oh Jesus, I forgive those who have reviled me, accused me, posted about me and attempted to assassinate my character. Oh Lord, what is the opinion of man in comparison to the glory of Your Presence? Am I now trying to please man or God? Let me be pleasing to You, oh God! Let my life be a living sacrifice that is holy and acceptable to You!

You are the light in all the earth! In You there is no darkness and I can trust you. Help my unbelief! Give me faith, eyes to see, and ears to hear. Direct my steps and cause me to walk in sync with You and You alone. Deliver me from the mouth of my accuser and put the enemy to open shame! You are God, Jesus! You are who I answer to. I love You, Lord. In Jesus name, amen!

Memory Verse

Blessed are you when others revile you and persecute you and utter all kinds of evil against you falsely on my account. (Matthew 5:11)

6

Prison

But the LORD was with Joseph and showed him steadfast love and gave him favor in the sight of the keeper of the prison. - Genesis 39:21

Favor isn't fair. It causes things to go well for the one who walks in it regardless of where said person finds themselves. Whether in a pit, as a slave, or wrongly imprisoned, nothing can stop the favor of God from finding you. The love and favor of God is upon those who love Him and do His will. He is with us and for us. We would do well to truly believe and accept that no matter where we find ourselves, God's favor will find us there. It is not something that is determined by the season around us, but rather God's favor causes the season we are in to bow to the King of all kings and the Lord of all lords! His favor is firm and resting.

Joseph was wrongfully imprisoned. It is likely that everyone surrounding Joseph believed his accuser, Potiphar's wife, and he was now left to sit in prison for a crime that he did not commit. As if sitting in prison for something you did not do was not bad enough, but also consider the actual character assassination that seemed to have worked. The people who may have once respected him and considered him to be a man of good report likely now considered him to be a man who violates innocent women. Let's pick up where we left off.

And Joseph's master took him and put him into the prison, the place where the king's prisoners were confined, and he was there in prison. But the LORD was with Joseph and showed him steadfast love and gave him favor in the sight of the keeper of the prison. And the keeper of the prison put Joseph in charge of all the prisoners who were in the prison. Whatever was done there, he was the one who did it. The keeper of the prison paid no attention to anything that was in Joseph's charge, because the LORD was with him. And whatever he did, the LORD made it succeed. - Genesis 39:20-23

Joseph was taken to the prison where the king's prisoners were confined. I want you to make a mental note of that, because we will look back at that in the next section.

I think sometimes we have an idea of what it will look like if God is truly with us. If we are honest, we assume that it will look like a prosperous life in every area and that is true, but sometimes

God so chooses to prosper us even while it looks like the accuser (the enemy) won the battle. Yet, God was with Joseph despite where he sat. It is so important that we deeply understand that God was with Joseph, in the prison. In the place of prevailing accusation and a false conviction of a crime he never committed.

God granted Joseph favor in the eyes of the keeper of the prison and again we see that someone in authority gives Joseph authority over all they are in charge of. Interesting parallel we see here. The keeper put Joseph in charge of all the prison, so much so that the keeper of the prison paid no attention to anything that Joseph was caring for. Again, we see Joseph getting in position for purpose. He has now stewarded all of Potiphar's house and the prison. Consider the skills he would have acquired by both of these seasons. To the world it looked like he was a slave and then a prisoner, but to the Lord he was being prepared to steward the known world and ensure God's people were saved.

Whatever Joseph did, the Lord made it succeed. Do we live believing that no matter what we do God makes it succeed? Even when it does not look like it is succeeding? I am sure Joseph did not feel like he was succeeding in prison. He was in a foreign land, rejected by his own brothers, a slave, and now a falsely convicted of rape. Could it be that God's idea of success and our idea of success are two totally different things? What if the anxiety we feel and the overwhelm we face is an indicator that our idea of how God moves and how He actually moves needs to be reconciled in our mind.

If we are honest, in the Instagram and TikTok era we are much more concerned with how things look than how they actually are. Could you sit in prison falsely accused and convicted and believe that God was with you and causing all that you were doing to succeed? I understand the implication of what I am saying here, but think about it. That is what happened in the life of Joseph. We are so consumed with filtered realities, vanity metrics and the acceptance of others that we actually believe that the approval of the masses is the approval of God. The success of the world and sadly, even the success of the church, isn't always the same as the success of heaven.

> TO PLEASE MAN IS TO LAY DOWN SERVANTHOOD TO CHRIST, TO PLEASE GOD IS TO LAY DOWN SERVANTHOOD OF MAN'S OPINION.

I have been saying this a lot in prayer lately, especially when I lead our church in corporate prayer, "get our eyes off of the success of the world/church and get our eyes on the success of heaven." Do we desire that people see us succeed, more than we desire for God to cause us to succeed? When our heart is for the success of heaven, more than the acceptance of man we can sit in the midst of it all knowing that God is with us and for us. It is an unshakable place. Just like we will see in the life of Joseph, time will always tell who is truly serving God. Mourning may happen in the night, but joy comes in the morning. The Apostle Paul said, "For am I now seeking the approval of man, or of God? Or am I trying to please man? If I were still trying to please man, I would not be a servant of Christ" (Galatians 1:10). Let us lay down the idea that the acceptance of man is the affirmation of God. To please man is to lay down servanthood to Christ, to please God is to lay down servanthood of man's opinion.

Gifts Come Alive Again

Some time after this, the cupbearer of the king of Egypt and his baker committed an offense against their lord the king of Egypt. And Pharaoh was angry with his two officers, the chief cupbearer and the chief baker, and he put them in custody in the house of the captain of the guard, in the prison where Joseph was confined. The captain of the guard appointed Joseph to be with them, and he attended them. They continued for some time in custody.

And one night they both dreamed—the cupbearer and the baker of the king of Egypt, who were confined in the prison—each his own dream, and each dream with its own interpretation. When Joseph came to them in the morning, he saw that they were troubled. So he asked Pharaoh's officers who were with him in custody in his master's house, "Why are your faces downcast today?" They said to him, "We have had dreams, and there is no one to interpret them." And Joseph said to them, "Do not interpretations belong to God? Please tell them to me."

So the chief cupbearer told his dream to Joseph and said to him, "In my dream there was a vine before me, and on the vine there were three branches. As soon as it budded, its blossoms shot forth, and the clusters ripened into grapes. Pharaoh's cup was in my hand, and I took the grapes and pressed them into Pharaoh's cup and placed the cup in Pharaoh's hand." Then Joseph said to him, "This is its interpretation: the three branches are three days. In three days Pharaoh will lift up your head and restore you to your office, and you shall place Pharaoh's cup in his hand as formerly, when you were his cupbearer. Only remember me, when it is well with you, and please do me the kindness to mention me to Pharaoh, and so get me out of this house. For I was indeed stolen out of the land of the Hebrews, and here also I have done nothing that they should put me into the pit."

When the chief baker saw that the interpretation was favorable, he said to Joseph, "I also had a dream: there were three cake baskets on my head, and in the uppermost basket there were all sorts of baked food for Pharaoh, but the birds were eating it out of the basket on my head." And Joseph answered and said, "This is its interpretation: the three baskets are three days. In three days Pharaoh will lift up your head— from you!—and hang you on a tree. And the birds will eat the flesh from you."

On the third day, which was Pharaoh's birthday, he made a feast for all his servants and lifted up the head of the chief cupbearer and the head of the chief baker among his servants. He

restored the chief cupbearer to his position, and he placed the cup in Pharaoh's hand. But he hanged the chief baker, as Joseph had interpreted to them. Yet the chief cupbearer did not remember Joseph, but forgot him.

- Genesis 40

If Joseph had not been in prison, he would not have been in a position to interpret the dreams of Pharaoh's servants who were imprisoned. Remember when I told you to take a mental note? He was imprisoned where the king's prisoners were kept, giving him access to people who would potentially have access to Pharaoh. Again, he was being put in position. Now whether or not Joseph had been dreaming or interpreting dreams before this moment, we do not know. This is the first time we see dreams or interpretation brought up again concerning Joseph since his original dreams that caused his brothers to throw him into the pit.

I just heard the Lord say, *"Just because it has been a little while since they operated in the giftings and callings that I have placed within them does not mean that they are gone or forgotten."*

Sometimes in the midst of the positioning it can seem like what God has given us is lying dormant. Some may feel like they are no longer gifted or that the calling has lifted, but that simply isn't true. When God gets you in the right place at the right time, God will cause what is within you to be seen around you. Just because you seem or even feel inactive for a season does not mean that God is done with you. I once heard someone say that, "gifting will take you where only character can sustain you." We often think that gifting is what is most needed to fulfill the call of

God on our lives, but really it is wisdom and character. The gifts are irrevocable (Romans 11:29). God can put a demand on the gifts whenever He desires, however wisdom and character are things that are gained through experience and life.

The beginning of wisdom is this: Get wisdom, and whatever you get, get insight. - Proverbs 4:7

When God is positioning us most of what we walk through is for the sake of gaining wisdom and growing in character. Yes, our gifts will surface when they are needed and as God desires to use them, but wisdom, integrity, and character will be needed to run the race, and finish the race well. When we desire to be used by God more than we desire to go through the process of God, we are headed for trouble and fast. Sure, we can elbow our way into what we are called to, but it is better to sit at the end of the table and be asked to move to the head than be asked to sit back at the end of the table.

He went on to tell a story to the guests around the table. Noticing how each had tried to elbow into the place of honor, he said, "When someone invites you to dinner, don't take the place of honor. Somebody more important than you might have been invited by the host. Then he'll come and call out in front of everybody, 'You're in the wrong place. The place of honor belongs to this man.' Embarrassed, you'll have to make your way to the very last table, the only place left.

When you're invited to dinner, go and sit at the last place. Then when the host comes he may very well say, 'Friend, come up to the front.' That will give the dinner guests something to talk about! What I'm saying is, If you walk around all high and mighty, you're going to end up flat on your face. But if you're content to be simply yourself, you will become more than yourself." - Luke 14:7-11, MSG

We can say with certainty that Joseph had gained much wisdom and equipping for what was to come. The gifts were surfacing again and he was drawing closer to finally stepping into purpose. He had been humbled in more ways than most of us can imagine and it seemed as though he would get out of prison soon.

After Two Whole Years... (Gen. 41:1a)

Yet the Bible tells us that Joseph waited another two years after correctly interpreting the dreams of the cupbearer and baker. Two years is a long time to wait on something, no matter how patient you are. Was that time wasted? Do you think that if God felt as though that time was wasted that He would have allowed Joseph to sit there for two more years? We know that God was with Joseph, we just read that. God had His eyes on Joseph, I mean God knew that He was going to move through Joseph to save the whole known world from a famine He had ordained. Then why did God let Joseph sit in prison for two more years? We don't know how long Joseph had been in prison prior to interpreting those dreams nor do we know how long Pharaoh's servants were in prison before their dreams. It could have been 4, 14, or even 40 years; we simply don't know.

But the Lord saw it fit that we know that after interpreting the dreams there were two whole additional years that he waited. I want to speak to those of you who feel like time has been wasted or like you are far behind. Time has not been wasted if you have been serving the Lord. Regardless of what that looks like on the outside. Whether it has the approval of man or the success of the world/church or not makes no difference at all to God. Many fear that years of their life have been wasted, but I would submit to you that if you love God and serve Him with your life that nothing in your life has or even can be wasted. He either uses all things for the good of those who love Him according to Romans 8:28 or God is a liar.

It is time that we truly reconcile what we say we believe with our reality and current moment. We believe that Jesus is the Lord and Savior, that He was born of a virgin, lived a sinless life and died on the cross providing the atonement of our sin, so we could be given access to a relationship with Father God. We believe that three days after He was crucified, He rose from the grave and conquered sin and death. Jesus is our Lord and our Savior. Friends, the Bible that tells us of this incredible work that Jesus did for us also tells us that God uses all things to the good of those who love Him.

And we know that for those who love God all things work together for good, for those who are called according to his purpose. - Romans 8:28

I believe what is holding many back from truly getting into position for purpose is this ambiguous timeline that we ourselves have set for when and how God is going to move. We would never communicate that we have this timeline, but if we are honest and take an inward look most of us feel this way. Zac (my husband) and I planted the church we pastor over six years ago. It would be easy for me to look at where our church is today and compare, not even to others around us, but to where I know God is taking us and become discouraged. The age-old question, "What am I doing wrong?", begins to creep in and if we are not careful we judge the season based off of our expectation and not off of what God has said.

TIME HAS NOT BEEN WASTED IF YOU HAVE BEEN SERVING THE LORD

Allow this word to go down deep into your belly and know that God did not find those two years of Joseph waiting as a waste, if He had He would have intervened. We don't know why God let him sit there for two more years, but we know that He did. Maybe you have been waiting for two years, maybe you have been waiting a lot longer, the principle remains the same; if God is with you and He is for you, you can find trust and deeply surrender to Him even in this season.

We cannot wait to trust Him when we are standing in the midst of purpose. We must trust Him long before our purpose is fulfilled. I would submit to you that the door to purpose opens when we submit to the positioning through fearless and abandoned trust in the Lord. You may very well come to a place or may be sitting in the place where you no longer care if you fulfill your purpose or not, not because you do not desire to be obedient to God, but because you have allowed the Lord to crucify that within you. You are in a good place, my friend. A seed must die in the ground before it sprouts to bare fruit.

Let's Pray

Father, thank you that you really do work all things together for my good. Thank you for healing every part of me that fears trusting you. Bring me closer to You and cause me to go deeper into Your word. Thank you, Lord, that as long as I am seeking You and serving You no time in my life is ever wasted. I love you, in Jesus name, amen.

Memory Verse

And we know that for those who love God all things work together for good, for those who are called according to his purpose. (Romans 8:28)

7

Promotion

And Pharaoh said to Joseph, "See, I have set you over all the land of Egypt." -Genesis 41:41

"I feel God saying that I am supposed to be connected to you in some way, here is my cell. Please give me a call when you are able." I was pretty stunned when I read that message as it came across my phone. I had no social media following, our church was tiny, I wasn't even sure if I believed it was okay to speak in tongues at church back then, yet Jenny Weaver was messaging me saying she felt God was telling her to connect with me. Me? Why me? I had very little to offer in the relationship. I was a stranger to her and while she was not a stranger to me, because I followed her social media so closely; we did not know each other.

When promotion comes, it seems sudden, but if you have been patient and waiting upon the Lord you will see that God has been preparing you for it all along. If you don't know who Jenny Weaver is, she is the senior leader of the Core Group, a mentorship group that is taking the world by storm. She is a worship leader, minister and revivalist. Her testimony is radical and can be found basically anywhere on the internet. The fact that she was messaging me blew my whole mind, but it did not stop there. Not only was Jenny asking me to help be a part of launching her Core Group Mentorship program (in 2018), but the publisher of Destiny Image, Larry Sparks, was also messaging me discussing how he could help me get my story out to the world and asking me to send him the book that I had been writing. No one even knew I was writing a book, yet God caused a publisher to reach out to me. I was writing Heal to Hear, by the way. Isn't God good?

> PROMOTION IS NEVER
> THE PURPOSE. IT IS THE
> CATALYST GOD USES.

As we see in the life of Joseph there is the season of rejection, preparation, promotion and then finally purpose. Promotion comes before purpose. We must heed the warning and expose the lie that promotion is the purpose. Promotion is never the purpose. It is the catalyst that God uses, so we are in position for purpose. Afterall, a slave/prisoner has no influence over how a global famine is stewarded, but a man second in command to the king sure does. God does not promote us to puff us up or allow us to believe that we are greater than the next, but rather He promotes us (however that looks in our individual lives) so that we can be in the right position when purpose comes.

We will look at all of this deeper in this chapter and in the coming chapters, but I want to share this right up front. Joseph was in the place of promotion for at least seven years before the purpose of his promotion was exposed. We know that there was seven years of abundance before there were seven years of famine, we do not know how long Joseph was in authority before the famine started, but we know he was in authority for at least seven years before the purpose of saving his family was brought about.

There is a danger when we camp out in promotion believing that it is because of what we have done or even worse simply because of who we are. God does not promote us so our resumes can look nice, so we can finally steward the greatest move of God the earth has ever seen or even anything close to that. God chooses to move through us, He does not have to. God promotes us when it is time and necessary for our purpose. How we steward the promotion will truly be the final test of if we will fulfill the purpose. When most people reach promotion they think they have arrived, this is the place, this is what all the waiting was for etc, etc., but if we fail to discern the promotion and why we have been promoted then when the purpose comes; we will miss it all together.

I would submit to you this is why we see some who have been promoted by God fall. God uses flawed men and women, He does not seek perfection before moving through someone's life. I mean David raped Bathsheba and murdered her husband to cover it up, still God called him a man after His own heart (see 1 Samuel 13:14). But if we misdiagnose the promotion we are left open to fall from a higher place. This is why it is imperative that we do not move ahead of God when it comes to promotion and

and purpose lest we fall from the pedestal that we built. God protects who He promotes.

When promotion hit my life, I was not ready for it. In fact, I was so unready that I had to pull back from it all together. You may say, "If God promotes me I know I am ready." Joseph was promoted in Potiphar's house and in the prison, yet he was not truly ready until Pharaoh dreamed. Discern the season through much prayer and fasting, so that by testing you will know the perfect will of God (Romans 12:2). The first time promotion entered into my life was in 2018, but I sit here writing this in 2022 knowing that I am just beginning to feel ready for what I am being positioned for. I still have a bit of positioning to go and I am fully submitted to that process with the Lord. Like Joseph God showed me the end from the beginning, it is how I steward and submit to God in these years of preparation that will determine if the end purpose is fulfilled. Let's dive back into the life of Joseph and watch how things change when he finally stands in promotion.

After two whole years, Pharaoh dreamed that he was standing by the Nile, and behold, there came up out of the Nile seven cows, attractive and plump, and they fed in the reed grass. And behold, seven other cows, ugly and thin, came up out of the Nile after them, and stood by the other cows on the bank of the Nile. And the ugly, thin cows ate up the seven attractive, plump cows. And Pharaoh awoke. And he fell asleep and dreamed a second time. And behold, seven ears of grain, plump and good, were growing on one stalk. And behold, after them sprouted seven

ears, thin and blighted by the east wind. And the thin ears swallowed up the seven plump, full ears. And Pharaoh awoke, and behold, it was a dream. So in the morning his spirit was troubled, and he sent and called for all the magicians of Egypt and all its wise men. Pharaoh told them his dreams, but there was none who could interpret them to Pharaoh. - Genesis 41:1-8

The Devil Can't Tell You What God is Doing

After receiving this dream from God, Pharaoh woke up troubled in his spirit. There is a lot that can be said about dream interpretation, but for the sake of our study together I won't go too deep into that. It mattered that his spirit was troubled, because that indicated that he needed to pay attention to dream and what it meant. It was also important that he had two dreams as Joseph will hit on when he interprets the dreams. Pharaoh called the magicians and the wise men, because it was believed that they could interpret dreams through dark arts.

Most people think that when the scripture is speaking of wise men it is speaking of men who were wise, but I invite you to do a deeper study of that independent from what I will share here. Wise men were diviners, not just men who were wise. That is why they are always grouped in with the magicians. Yes, this includes the wise men who gave gifts to Jesus. I know, the Christmas story that you've heard preached for years isn't actually that accurate. Go study it for yourself.

It is interesting though that they could not interpret the dreams because God had hidden its meaning from the demonic spirits. Remember what Joseph said to the cupbearer and the baker, "Do interpretations not belong to God?" (Genesis 40:8). When God speaks you will not be able to discern or interpret what has been said through natural or demonic means, God alone will be able to speak on behalf of what He said, because He is the one who said it. God was putting Joseph in position yet again, by showing Pharaoh that Joseph, because of the God he served, had the upper hand over the magicians and wise men.

Then the chief cupbearer said to Pharaoh, "I remember my offenses today. When Pharaoh was angry with his servants and put me and the chief baker in custody in the house of the captain of the guard, we dreamed on the same night, he and I, each having a dream with its own interpretation. A young Hebrew was there with us, a servant of the captain of the guard. When we told him, he interpreted our dreams to us, giving an interpretation to each man according to his dream. And as he interpreted to us, so it came about. I was restored to my office, and the baker was hanged."

Then Pharaoh sent and called Joseph, and they quickly brought him out of the pit. And when he had shaved himself and changed his clothes, he came in before Pharaoh. - Genesis 41:9-14

The cupbearer remembered Joseph, when it was time. What Joseph did in interpreting their dreams was not done in vain, even though the man forgot for over two years. It may seem as though some things were done in vain, things that you know God told you to do and you knew would lead to His purpose being fulfilled in your life. Though it looks like it was in vain, it wasn't! In the right time God will bring it to remembrance. You didn't miss it, God just has perfect timing.

"For My thoughts are not your thoughts, neither are your ways My ways," declares the LORD. "For as the heavens are higher than the earth, so My ways are higher than your ways and My thoughts than your thoughts." - Isaiah 55:8-9

Did you catch where it said they brought Joseph from? The pit. Talk about a full circle moment. They brought Joseph from the pit to stand in front of Pharaoh. The pit was the first place of rejection from his brothers, the place of exposure from covering, the place where favor (the coat of many colors) had been stripped from him, the place that was second best to dead had now been redeemed as the place where God was with him, where God showed him steadfast love and was now the place that positioned him for purpose. Though he was in this pit, the prison, for false accusation, God moved and showed His favor to be greater than any accusation that could ever be thrown at him. They drew him out of the pit quickly, when promotion comes it will seem sudden although it was many, many years in the making.

And Pharaoh said to Joseph, "I have had a dream, and there is no one who can interpret it. I have heard it said of you that when you hear a dream you can interpret it." Joseph answered

Pharaoh, "It is not in me; God will give Pharaoh a favorable answer." Then Pharaoh said to Joseph, "Behold, in my dream I was standing on the banks of the Nile. Seven cows, plump and attractive, came up out of the Nile and fed in the reed grass. Seven other cows came up after them, poor and very ugly and thin, such as I had never seen in all the land of Egypt. And the thin, ugly cows ate up the first seven plump cows, but when they had eaten them no one would have known that they had eaten them, for they were still as ugly as at the beginning. Then I awoke. I also saw in my dream seven ears growing on one stalk, full and good. Seven ears, withered, thin, and blighted by the east wind, sprouted after them, and the thin ears swallowed up the seven good ears. And I told it to the magicians, but there was no one who could explain it to me."

Then Joseph said to Pharaoh, "The dreams of Pharaoh are one; God has revealed to Pharaoh what he is about to do. The seven good cows are seven years, and the seven good ears are seven years; the dreams are one. The seven lean and ugly cows that came up after them are seven years, and the seven empty ears blighted by the east wind are also seven years of famine. It is as I told Pharaoh; God has shown to Pharaoh what he is about to do. There will come seven years of great plenty throughout all the land of Egypt, but after them there will arise seven years of famine, and all the plenty will be forgotten in the land of Egypt. **The famine will consume the land, and the plenty will be unknown in the land by reason of the famine that will follow, for it will be very severe. And the doubling of Pharaoh's dream means that the thing is fixed by God, and God will shortly bring it about. Now therefore let Pharaoh select a discerning and wise man, and set him over the land of Egypt. Let Pharaoh proceed to appoint overseers over the land and take one-fifth of the produce of the land of Egypt during the seven plentiful years. And let them gather all the food of these good years that are coming and store up grain under the authority of Pharaoh for food in the cities, and let them keep it. That food shall be a reserve for the land against the seven years of famine that are to occur in the land of Egypt, so that the land may not perish through the famine."**

- Genesis 41:15-36

Humility is Key

The very first words out of Joseph's mouth as he steps into promotion is, "It is not me; God will," may those words ring through our spirit and reverberate with heaven. It is not me, God will. Joseph did not say, "Yes, I can interpret dreams because I am a dream interpreter." No, in total humility and submission to God, he acknowledged that it was not him at all. It was God alone. The season of promotion demands that you know it was never you at all, but only God alone. The second that you begin to think it is because of you, because of your gift, because of your testimony or your anointing is the moment the promotion becomes the place of pride and pride is what comes before a fall (Proverbs 16:18).

Again, so much to be taught here about dream interpretation, but I want to camp out on the fact that Joseph did not stop at interpreting the dream of Pharaoh. He also gave a word of wisdom on how to steward the warning that God gave Pharaoh. Many think the power behind the prophetic is discerning the warnings and judgements of God, but the prophetically mature know that when God gives a warning He also provides instruction.

God was not leaving the people to die, but rather He was telling them what was to take place, so that they could be in position for what He was doing. We now see that God was positioning a man for purpose, so that a nation could be positioned for their purpose. If Egypt had not heeded the word of the Lord through Joseph, the known world would have died. This famine would be a global famine and by the end the only place in the known world to get food was Egypt (see Gen 41:57). While what God is doing in and through us impacts us, it is so much greater than just us and our lives.

Heed or Intercede

Another radical principle that we charismatics and pentecostals would do good to learn from this passage is that some warnings are fixed by God. Oftentimes when God gives us or a prophet a warning, we begin to pray and intercede for God to change His mind. There are seasons when we need to heed while there are other seasons when we need to intercede. Discernment and seeking the Lord will show us which season we are in. Joseph told Pharaoh that because he had the dream twice it meant that the thing was fixed and would come to pass quickly. Rather than calling Egypt to pray and fast, God was calling them to prepare because His mind was made up on the matter.

Recently in my business God spoke to me and told me that my business would take a turn and finances would change for a time. During the time of Him telling me this my business was in the greatest season it had ever been in. I did not discern that God had fixed this to happen and my intercessions were not only unnecessary, but they would not change His mind on the matter. He told me not to hire anyone else and to prepare for what was to come. I, in my ignorance, thought this was a call to intercede rather than heed. I began to pray every day, but I moved forward in my business as usual.

It spiraled into the hardest financial season I have faced in many years, but I was not without understanding as God had already spoken to me. The sheer irony is, God was slowing my business down so I had more than enough time to write this book and He wanted to ensure that I had the money to sustain my family and business while I took this time away. I have since repented and learned a valuable lesson. In God's mercy He has sustained my family and my business, but I am not sitting in the abundance that I should have been because I did not heed the word.

This proposal pleased Pharaoh and all his servants. And Pharaoh said to his servants, "Can we find a man like this, in whom is the Spirit of God?" Then Pharaoh said to Joseph, "Since God has shown you all this, there is none so discerning and wise as you are. You shall be

This proposal pleased Pharaoh and all his servants. And Pharaoh said to his servants, "Can we find a man like this, in whom is the Spirit of God?" Then Pharaoh said to Joseph, "Since God has shown you all this, there is none so discerning and wise as you are. You shall be over my house, and all my people shall order themselves as you command. Only as regards the throne will I be greater than you." And Pharaoh said to Joseph, "See, I have set you over all the land of Egypt." Then Pharaoh took his signet ring from his hand and put it on Joseph's hand, and clothed him in garments of fine linen and put a gold chain about his neck. And he made him ride in his second chariot. And they called out before him, "Bow the knee!" Thus he set him over all the land of Egypt. Moreover, Pharaoh said to Joseph, "I am Pharaoh, and without your consent no one shall lift up hand or foot in all the land of Egypt." And Pharaoh called Joseph's name Zaphenath-paneah. And he gave him in marriage Asenath, the daughter of Potiphera Priest of On. So Joseph went out over the land of Egypt. - Genesis 41:37-45

Prisoner to Governor

In an instant, Joseph went from being a prisoner to governor (Gen 42:6). Pharaoh recognized that the Spirit of God was within Joseph and said there was none more discerning than him in all the land, asserting God's authority over all demonic spirits that would have been speaking to Pharaoh through magicians and diviners as was custom in Egypt. Joseph was put in charge of all of Pharaoh's house, all the people and over all the land of Egypt. Doesn't this sound familiar? Yet again, Joseph is put in charge of everything, literally everything. All the time of preparation, preparing and practicing was now paying off and possibly even making sense. It was finally time to put all the skills that he learned in Potiphar's house and in the prison to work.

Pharaoh took his signet ring and put it on Joseph's hand and clothed him in garments of fine linen. What was stolen from Joseph when he was thrown into the pit by his brothers? His coat of many colors, the fine linen that clothed him, and here he stands clothed in fine linens, the signet ring of the king and gold jewelry. Nothing that was stolen was lost. How true is this for our lives? Nothing that the enemy stole will stay gone forever. No, in fact God will not only restore what was taken but He will provide restitution, seven times more, for all that the enemy stole (Prov 6:31).

Let's Pray

Jesus, let me stay in perfect step with You! Never getting ahead and never falling behind. Lord, I repent of when I went ahead of You or complained in the waiting. Help me lean into what you are teaching me and learn all that I need to steward the season of promotion and purpose well. Give me wisdom oh God that I might run the race well and finish with excellence. I love you, Lord! Who can do the mighty works that you do, but you alone? You are God! My God! Help me to walk in humility and give all the glory to you. You are worthy of all glory, all praise and all honor. In Jesus name, amen.

Memory Verse

For My thoughts are not your thoughts, neither are your ways My ways," declares the LORD. "For as the heavens are higher than the earth, so My ways are higher than your ways and My thoughts than your thoughts. (Isaiah 55:8-9)

8

Purpose Begins

So ten of Joseph's brothers went down to buy grain in Egypt.
- Genesis 42:3

"I heard the Lord say look around, do you see all that surrounds you?" I looked around the 700+ sanctuary, knowing that the church had a little over a thousand people in attendance on Sunday's. I said, "Yes I see what surrounds me." The man spoke and said, "The Lord said He is about to remove your veil and the world will see you, for He will be the one to remove your veil." The prophet went on to prophesy a life defining word from the Lord over my life, one that has given every step that I have taken purpose. I choose not to type it here in this book as I do not lack wisdom. One day, I'll share the whole word. Nonetheless the word marked me forever, I mean I was only a few weeks sober if that. When I tell this story I joke and say I probably still smelt like weed when this prophet spoke this word over me.

The things the prophet spoke were powerful and life changing, yet I stood here (much like 17 year old Joseph) thinking, "What!?" The most incredible part is what happened next. Shortly after this moment I reconnected with Zac. Within four short months, I was standing on the bank of Lake Washington in a wedding dress saying my vows to Zac. The wind was especially intense as a big storm had just rolled in. In our wedding video you can hear the sirens going off and visibly see that it was pouring down rain. We didn't care. We did not care in the slightest, we were in love and just ecstatic to be married. We stood there alone, with no family or friends surrounding us. Just us, the pastor, and random people the pastor had invited. Really funny to think about now, but we could have cared less. We weren't getting married for any other reason than God told us to and we were in love. It wasn't about the glitz or the glam, I've seen weddings that cost more than a house end in adultery and divorce not even six months later.

It was about God and us. That is all our lives have ever been about. When it came time for me to read my vows, I stared into Zac's stunning green eyes and shook. Partly because I was soaking wet and freezing cold, but also because I knew my life was just beginning. As the words of my vows crossed my lips something extraordinary happened. The wind blew just right, lifting my veil off of my face and revealing it to Zac. The wind blew so hard that it actually took my veil off of my head and blew it into Lake Washington. The Lord said that He would lift my veil and He did, He is and was my groom first; He revealed me to my husband and in that moment I realized that the Lord Himself had walked me down the aisle to my groom. I knew that all that the prophet had spoken that day would come to pass. At that moment, I knew the purpose for my life had been set and fixed by God.

Purpose is something that no one, but God can give you. It is a driving force in your life and if you allow it, it will produce within you endurance, stamina and a grace to endure no matter what life throws at you. When you have a strong sense of purpose, life makes sense. When you lack purpose or understanding of your purpose, life can derail you easily and getting back on course will be harder. When things happen in my life that hurt or things that I do not expect get thrown my way, it may for a moment cause me to pause, but I always get back up and keep going because I know my purpose. In the business world this idea has been adapted to "my why." You hear this a lot in network marketing especially. The idea is if you know the why behind why you do what you do, the why will cause you to push past the insecurity, doubt, etc.

PURPOSE IS SOMETHING THAT NO ONE BUT GOD CAN GIVE YOU

For example, if your reason for building a business is so you can step away from an unfulfilling desk job, when you do not desire to show up for your business and share what you are selling, remember your why and allow that to push you past the momentary discomfort. Purpose is similar, but oh so much deeper. Purpose causes you to push back more than momentary discomfort, it propels you and causes things to make sense. In my life, I have had extreme and crazy things happen such as a group of witches sacrificing a pig in my backyard. Yes, that really happened. Yes, I have photos to prove it. The police and animal control said it was the most heinous crime they had ever seen committed against an animal and told us if they caught who did it they would go to prison. In the natural, that seemed so odd and out there. We had a tiny church of about thirty at the time, no one really knew who we were and it did not seem like we were making that big of an impact. But in the spirit, I knew exactly why that happened. The warfare is a prophecy, remember? That warfare did not speak of where we currently were, but it was certainly telling a story of where we were going. I know my purpose, so when bizarre things happen that seem so outlandish for where I currently am; I am aware of why. Only God's purpose and understanding of God's purpose for your life can give you that kind of fortitude and stamina to endure.

What is Your Purpose?

What is your purpose in life? This is a question that most people ask themselves, yet few find an answer to. People who know the answer to this question seem to live happier, more fulfilled lives, while those who fail to truly lay hold of their life's purpose seem to go through the motions with a "the chips fall where they may" sort of attitude. Purpose can drive you when inspiration fails. Purpose will cause you to keep going even when everything around you says to stop. In this chapter, we will begin to see everything start to make more sense in the life of Joseph as his true purpose is revealed. I pray that as we study this and you ponder your life's purpose and God's vision for your life that it will cause you to go deeper into your relationship with the Lord to inquire and understand the true purpose of your life. I am a firm believer that the Bible is true, you may have noticed that by now. If the Bible is true, then we do not have to fear not having a purpose or worse fear that God will not tell us our purpose.

> 'Call to Me and I will answer you, and tell you [and even show you] great and mighty things, [things which have been confined and hidden], which you do not know and understand and cannot distinguish.' - Jeremiah 33:3, AMP

Maybe right now your purpose is a great and hidden thing that you don't know, but God said if you call to Him He will answer you and tell you the things that have been previously hidden and the things that you could not distinguish. Understanding the purpose of your life is the entire purpose of this book and I believe without a shadow of a doubt that, like Joseph, you will both know and fulfill the purpose of God in your life. It does not matter if you are seventeen or seventy, God can and He will begin to move as you seek His face in this matter. I am so excited for you. Let's pick up where we left off as Joseph begins to step fully into his purpose.

> Joseph was thirty years old when he entered the service of Pharaoh, king of Egypt. And Joseph went out from the presence of Pharaoh and went through all the land of Egypt. During the seven plentiful years the earth produced abundantly, and he gathered up all the food of these seven years, which occurred in the land of Egypt, and put the food in the cities. He put in every city the food from the fields around it. And Joseph stored up grain in great abundance, like the sand of the sea, until he ceased to measure it, for it could not be measured.

Joseph was thirty years old when he entered the service of Pharaoh, king of Egypt. And Joseph went out from the presence of Pharaoh and went through all the land of Egypt. During the seven plentiful years the earth produced abundantly, and he gathered up all the food of these seven years, which occurred in the land of Egypt, and put the food in the cities. He put in every city the food from the fields around it. And Joseph stored up grain in great abundance, like the sand of the sea, until he ceased to measure it, for it could not be measured.

Before the year of famine came, two sons were born to Joseph. Asenath, the daughter of Potiphera priest of On, bore them to him. Joseph called the name of the first born Manasseh. "For," he said, "God has made me forget all my hardship and all my father's house." The name of the second he called Ephraim, "For God has made me fruitful in the land of my affliction."

The seven years of plenty that occurred in the land of Egypt came to an end, and the seven years of famine began to come, as Joseph had said. There was famine in all lands, but in all the land of Egypt there was bread. When all the land of Egypt was famished, the people cried to Pharaoh for bread. Pharaoh said to all the Egyptians, "Go to Joseph. What he says to you, do."

So when the famine had spread over all the land, Joseph opened all the store houses and sold to the Egyptians, for the famine was severe in the land of Egypt. Moreover, all the earth came to Egypt to Joseph to buy grain, because the famine was severe over all the earth. - Genesis 41:46-57

Promotion Will Be Forgotten

Promotion won't be remembered, but purpose will. Isn't it interesting that the Bible shares such in depth details of when Joseph was afflicted, yet during his (at least) seven years of promotion while he was storing up for the famine we get such few details. Sure, we get the details of his wife and his sons, but that isn't abnormal culturally to record the wife and children. Remember when I said the purpose is not the promotion, but promotion will get you in position for purpose? We really see that ringing true in this passage, the promotion isn't a focal point here at all, but the impending purpose is.

We see this even today, many people are promoted, they hold positions of fame and even influence, but only those who fulfill a purpose and make an impact are remembered. To further that point even more there are many who only their purpose and impact are remembered while they themselves are forgotten all together. Do you know who started the Salvation Army? I do, but it is likely that you don't yet it still stands today. Do you enjoy evangelistic church where you live? Do you know who brought that great reform from Catholicism? Maybe you do, but many do not, yet they enjoy the benefits of Martin Luther's purpose being fulfilled nonetheless. Do you know the life story of the man who created the internet? Could you tell any facts about the man that created the iPhone? Maybe you know the answers to all these questions, but most could not. Promotion comes, but it is not what will be remembered; fulfilled purpose is what will be remembered.

All the Earth

All of the earth was impacted by the famine, the entire earth. Could you even fathom God placing you in a position where you had to steward the food supply for the entire earth? I couldn't, that is simply hard to even imagine, much less comprehend. It blows my mind to really think of all that Joseph endured leading up to these moments, he was rejected by his family, sold as a slave, unjustly imprisoned and now the entire earth was dependent upon whether or not he saved enough food for all of them to live.

While I am not asserting that if you had a hard life it must mean you will rule over the entire world's food supply, I am also not going to overlook the severity of what Joseph endured compared to the severity that the world was now enduring. What if all those hardships were pointing to purpose? What if...? Open our eyes to see oh Lord that we may see what You are doing on the earth! Give us ears to hear oh Lord that we may hear and have understanding of what You are saying!

When Jacob learned that there was grain for sale in Egypt, he said to his sons, "Why do you look at one another?" And he said, "Behold, I have heard that there is grain for sale in Egypt. Go down and buy grain for us there, that we may live and not die." So ten of Joseph's brothers went down to buy grain in Egypt. But

Jacob did not send Benjamin, Joseph's brother, with his brothers, for he feared that harm might happen to him. Thus the sons of Israel came to buy among the others who came, for the famine was in the land of Canaan.

Now Joseph was governor over the land. He was the one who sold to all the people of the land. And Joseph's brothers came and bowed themselves before him with their faces to the ground. Joseph saw his brothers and recognized them, but he treated them like strangers and spoke roughly to them. "Where do you come from?" he said. They said,"From the land of Canaan, to buy food." And Joseph recognized his brothers, but they didn't recognize him. And Joseph remembered the dreams that he had dreamed of them. And he said to them, "You are spies; you have come to see the nakedness of the land." They said to him, "No, my lord, your servants have come to buy food. 11 We are all sons of one man. We are honest men. Your servants have never been spies."

He said to them, "No, it is the nakedness of the land that you have come to see." And they said, "We, your servants, are twelve brothers, the sons of one man in the land of Canaan, and behold, the youngest is this day with our father, and one is no more." But Joseph said to them, "It is as I said to you. You are spies. By this you shall be tested: by the life of Pharaoh, you shall not go from this place unless your youngest brother comes here. Send one of you, and let him bring your brother, while you remain confined, that your words may be tested, whether there is truth in you. Or else, by the life of Pharaoh, surely you are spies." And he put them all together in custody for three days.

On the third day Joseph said to them, "Do this and you will live, for I fear God: if you are honest men, let one of your brothers remain confined where you are in custody, and let the rest go and carry grain for the famine of your households, and bring your youngest brother to me. So your words will be verified, and you shall not die." And they did so. Then they said to one another, "In truth we are guilty concerning our brother, in that we saw the distress of his soul, when he begged us and we did not listen. That is why this distress has come upon us." And Reuben answered them, "Did I not tell you not to sin against the boy? But you did not listen. So now there comes a reckoning for his blood." They did not know that Joseph understood them, for there was an interpreter between them. Then he turned away from them and wept. And he returned to them and spoke to them. And he took Simeon from them and bound him before their eyes. And Joseph gave orders to fill their bags with grain, and to replace every man's money in his sack, and to give them provisions for the journey. This was done for them.

- Genesis 42:1-25

Purpose Key: Vengeance is Mine

Nothing will derail purpose faster than taking matters into our own hands. Never one time did Joseph take things into his own hands, but rather he trusted God throughout it all. The Bible tells us that vengeance belongs to the Lord, we are told to never avenge ourselves, but to leave it to the wrath of God, because He will repay (see Rom 12:19). God's vengeance and our vengeance are two totally different things. When someone has wronged us and we seek vengeance, we usually desire that the person who afflicted us will feel what we felt or go through what we went through. God's vengeance is much, much deeper than that. Rather than a moment of affliction that yields nothing but pain, God's vengeance is a deep work that brings men and women to repentance. When we allow God to fight the battle, in the end God will be glorified. If we fight the battle, in the end we will be hurt.

Sometimes we think that God thinks like us, but that could not be further from the truth. What good would it have been if God would have thrown all of Joseph's brothers into a pit and sold them all into slavery too? Would we even know the twelve tribes of Israel if that had been the case? Has that crossed your mind yet, that the men who threw Joseph into the pit are the other eleven tribes of Israel? God's people, the descents of Abraham, the lineage that Jesus would be birthed from. These men were God's people; Jehovah, The God of Abraham, Isaac and Jacob (Gen 50:24). Jacob, who was renamed Israel, was Joseph's father. God would in fact repay the brothers of Joseph, but in a way that only God could.

Isn't it so telling that the brothers knew what they were

enduring was because of what they had done to Joseph? They said that the affliction they were facing was a reckoning for the blood of Joseph. I wonder what made them say that or how often they had thought about Joseph and what they had done to him prior to this moment. There is a lesson in this for us and that is this; sometimes it looks like those who have afflicted us have the upper hand but there will be a reckoning and like Joseph's brothers they will know why God's vengeance has come upon them.

As new testament believers, we often like to think that God does not repay with vengeance anymore, but friend that is a fallacy that has come in under the hyper grace umbrella, none of which is backed by scripture. Galatians 6:7 says, "Do not be deceived: God is not mocked, for whatever one sows, that will he also reap." Even Jesus said...

Judge not, and you will not be judged; condemn not, and you will not be condemned; forgive, and you will be forgiven; give, and it will be given to you. Good Measure, pressed down, shaken together, running over, will be put into your lap. For with the measure you use it will be measured back to you." - Luke 6:37-38

We will reap what we sow in this life. If we sow discord, we will reap discord. If we sow peace, we will reap righteousness (James 3:18). God is watching how we treat others and the expectation and standard that we are held to is that of the Word, not what your preacher has preached to you. Do you hear me? Let that sink deep down into your belly. If your preacher preaches something contrary to the Word of God to you, he will be held accountable for that; that is why he is doubly accountable. He is accountable for his life and for what he preaches (see James 3:1). But make no mistake, you will be held accountable for the Word of God. Standing before God saying, "well my preacher said," will not exempt you from being held accountable to what the Word of God says.

Purpose Key: Bless Your Enemies

Walking in purpose will require you to bless your enemies. Joseph knew what his brothers were saying, he understood them because there was an interpreter. Joseph knew what they were enduring mentally and emotionally, the vengeance of the Lord, yet Joseph repaid them with good. He filled their moneybags up with their money and gave them more than enough to feed them and their family. Yes, Joseph bound Simeon and kept him, but I would submit to you that he did so to ensure they returned to him. He did speak harshly to them, possibly because of emotion or maybe he actually thought they were there to spy. We don't know, but with him blessing his brothers and not taking their money I believe it is safe to assume that he took care of Simeon while he was in his care and fed him well. After all the evil that they had committed against Joseph, he blessed them. This reminds me of the words of Jesus…

"But I say to you who hear, Love your enemies, do good to those who hate you, bless those who curse you, pray for those who abuse you. To one who strikes you on the cheek, offer the other also, and from one who takes away your cloak do not withhold your tunic either. Give to everyone who begs from you, and from one who takes away your goods do not demand them back. And

as you wish that others would do to you, do so to them.

"If you love those who love you, what benefit is that to you? For even sinners love those who love them. And if you do good to those who do good to you, what benefit is that to you? For even sinners do the same. And if you lend to those from whom you expect to receive, what credit is that to you? Even sinners lend to sinners, to get back the same amount. But love your enemies, and do good, and lend, expecting nothing in return, and your reward will be great, and you will be sons of the Most High, for he is kind to the ungrateful and the evil. Be merciful, even as your Father is merciful. - Luke 6:27-36

Joseph repaid them by blessing them. He loved his brothers and blessed them even though they desired to murder him. In my own life I have found that obeying this scripture is a profound act of love toward God and to people. Bless those who curse you. It is not uncommon for me to bless those who curse me with gifts and verbal blessings. It keeps my heart pure before the Lord and withholds my soul from offense. There is a man who is set against me and has been for the last nine years, he posts vile evil about me and tries with all he can to defame my character. So, you know what I have done to repay him? I have sown into his ministry, I paid for him and his wife to go on a vacation and much more over the years. I am not doing this to win his approval, but rather I am doing this to keep my heart pure before God. I repay his evil with good, because that is what God has called us to do.

It is sad that I have to clarify this, but because of how this passage has been manipulated I want to add this. I do not allow this person in my home, access to me, my family or my social media profiles or anything of the sort; it says pray for those who abuse you. He is very abusive toward me, so I pray and bless from a distance. It is sad how even in the marriage covenant people have twisted these verses to further their agenda and not the heart of the Father. If you are being abused, you need to separate yourself from your abuser. Married or not and I do not care how much backlash I get for this, the Bible is very clear on how husbands are to treat their wives and wives you do not have to stay under the same roof as someone who hits or abuses you. I am not advocating the first step is divorce though it very well may end in divorce if they refuse to repent of physically abusing you, but I am certainly saying you have biblical grounds to ensure that you and your children are safe. Do not allow a manipulation of the Bible to cause you to stay in abuse, that is not God's will or the truth of His Word. If you or someone you know is being abused, please call the National Domestic Violence Hotline. Hours: 24/7. Languages: English, Spanish and 200+ through interpretation service. You can call 800-799-7233, text START to 88788 or visit their website at thehotline.org.

Get in Position

Joseph blessed them and he remembered his dream as they were bowing down to him. Purpose was beginning, the physical salvation of God's people. The events of his life came to a culmination as Joseph stood over them. It was time for Joseph to fully step into God's purpose for his life and in order to do that he had to: 1. Trust God to repay & 2. Bless and forgive his enemies.

Are you ready to step into purpose? Are you truly ready to let go of the aimless walk and step into what God has created you to do? Then it is time to let God do the repaying and bless/forgive your enemies. Forgiving your enemies is not for their sake. It does not say what they did to you was okay. No, in fact it's quite the opposite. It is saying that you are okay, in spite of all they did to you. Forgiveness is for you. God will handle them, however He sees fit, you need only worry about being in right standing with Father God. Are you ready to forgive your enemies? If so, friend you truly are positioned for purpose.

Let's Pray

Father, I desire to live in purpose, so that I can live on purpose. From this day forward I do not desire to just go through the motions aimlessly. I want to know my purpose and walk in it with full confidence. I forgive those who have cursed me. I forgive those who hate me. I forgive those who have abused me. I forgive them! I forgive them! I let the pain go, I lay it at Your feet. I let the replaying of it in my mind over and over go right now in Jesus name! Vindicate me oh God! Set me free from the bondage of unforgiveness so I can walk into Your purpose for my life right now.

Whatever you have for my life, Lord, whether I know it, partially know it or have no idea, help me to get into position so that I can walk it out. Help me forgive and bless! I call upon the name of Jesus for help! Help me, Lord! Help me hear You and obey You. Give me wisdom and understanding. Give me eyes to see and ears to hear. Jesus... I cannot do this without You, I cannot do this in my own strength! I lean on You! I push past the crowd, I lay down my agenda, I WANT YOU JESUS! I just want You. I love You! In Jesus name, amen.

Make sure you are following along in your Joseph: Positioned for Purpose Workbook as we dive deep in finding your purpose to go along with this chapter.

Memory Verse

Call to me and I will answer you, and will tell you great and hidden things that you have not known. (Jeremiah 33:3)

9

Goshen

The land of Egypt is before you. Settle Your father and your brothers in the best of the land. Let them settle in the land of Goshen. - Genesis 47:6

All of our time together has led up to these moments and while I have a lot to say about this portion of scripture, reading all of it in preparation for writing this chapter brought me to tears. I believe it is best if we read the full story and then discuss some elements more in depth after. Warning! If you are a crier, get some tissue, because after all the study we have put in these passages are incredibly moving.

Then Joseph could not control himself before all those who stood by him. He cried, "Make everyone go out from me." So no one stayed with him when Joseph made himself known to his brothers. And he wept aloud, so that the Egyptians heard it, and the household of Pharaoh heard it. And Joseph said to his brothers, "I am Joseph! Is my father still alive?" But his brothers could not answer him, for they were dismayed at his presence.

So Joseph said to his brothers, "Come near to me, please." And they came near. And he said, "I am your brother, Joseph, whom you sold into Egypt. And now do not be distressed or angry with yourselves because you sold me here, for God sent me before you to preserve life. For the famine has been in the land these two years, and there are yet five years in which there will be neither plowing nor harvest. And God sent me before you to preserve for you a remnant on earth, and to keep alive for you many survivors.
- Genesis 45:1-7

God Sent Me

Joseph wept so loud that the Egyptians and the household of Pharaoh heard it. Have you ever wept aloud like that? I know that I have. Sometimes the most spiritual thing you can do is cry and cry hard. Imagine all that Joseph must have been letting go as he wept on his brothers. It all finally made sense. The overwhelm of what Joseph felt had to have been great. I hear the Lord saying,

"Cry aloud for your breakthrough has come! Shed with tears the sorrow of these last several years for I AM with you and I AM for you. I will bring you into a place of understanding. What you have endured is not in vain, I will bring my glory out of the ashes."

I feel the Holy Ghost even just writing this! Joseph began to comfort them, knowing that God had sent him there. Imagine looking your "enemy" in the face, the one who stripped you, threw you in the pit and lied about your whereabouts and saying, "God sent me before you to preserve you." What great maturity and fortitude that takes. I pray that we are the people who can see that though the enemy moved, God stepped in and caused the hardest moments to become the moments that set us up for position in our purpose. I pray that we are people who have such a fearless trust in God that no matter what may happen in this life, we are steadfast and firm. What a deliverance from worry! When you truly know and believe that God will bring purpose out of what was meant to kill us.

So it was not you who sent me here, but God. He has made me a father to Pharaoh, and lord of all his house and ruler over all the land of Egypt. Hurry and go up to my father and say to him, 'Thus says your son Joseph, God has made me lord of all Egypt. Come down to me; do not tarry. You shall dwell in the land of Goshen, and you shall be near me, you and your children and your children's children, and your flocks, your herds, and all that you have. There I will provide for you, for there are yet five years of famine to come, so that you and your household, and all

that you have, do not come to poverty.' And now your eyes see, and the eyes of my brother Benjamin see, that it is my mouth that speaks to you. You must tell my father of all my honor in Egypt, and of all that you have seen. Hurry and bring my father down here." Then he fell upon his brother Benjamin's neck and wept, and Benjamin wept upon his neck And he kissed all his brothers and wept upon them. After that his brothers talked with him.

When the report was heard in Pharaoh's house, "Joseph's brothers have come," it pleased Pharaoh and his servants. And Pharaoh said to Joseph, "Say to your brothers, 'Do this: load your beasts and go back to the land of Canaan, and take your father and your households, and come to me, and I will give you the best of the land of Egypt, and you shall eat the fat of the land.' And you, Joseph, are commanded to say, 'Do this: take wagons from the land of Egypt for your little ones and for your wives, and bring your father, and come. Have no concern for your goods, for the best of all the land of Egypt is yours.'

The sons of Israel did so: and Joseph gave them wagons, according to the command of Pharaoh, and gave them provisions for the journey. To each and all of them he gave a change of clothes, but to Benjamin he gave three hundred shekels of silver and five changes of clothes. To his

**father he sent as follows: ten donkeys loaded
with the good things of Egypt, and ten female
donkeys loaded with grain, bread, and provision
for his father on the journey. Then he sent his
brothers away, and as they departed, he said to
them, "Do not quarrel on the way."**

- Genesis 45:8-24

A Land of Plenty

Goshen [goh-shuhn] : a pastoral region in Lower Egypt,
occupied by the Israelites before the Exodus; a land or place of
plenty and comfort. [4]

Israel and his family were leaving a place of famine and lack
to come into a place of plenty and comfort. Goshen was the best
land in all of Egypt, suitable for crop and livestock. It was a safe
place in the midst of all that was happening to the world. In so
many ways it is a prophetic depiction of God's protection over
His people no matter what the world faces. It was a place of
refuge and shelter. They passed from a place that was sure to
yield death, because of the great famine that had covered the
earth, into a place that would do more than just meet their needs.
Goshen was a place of prosperity and rapid growth for Israel and
his family. Goshen was the place where Israel and his sons went
from being a large family to becoming a great nation.

Israel and his sons entered into Goshen and when Moses
brought the people out of Egypt they were great in multitudes,
they were the great nation that had been promised. Make no
mistake that God can and He will protect His people even in the

---

4 "DICTIONARY.COM," Collins English Dictionary - Complete & Unabridged 2012 Digital
Edition, January 5, 2023, https://www.dictionary.com/browse/goshen.

midst of a worldwide crisis. The Lord has for us a Goshen even now, but much greater than a physical location we have an eternal relationship with Jesus Christ. Jesus is our refuge, our strength, our ever present help in our times of need. Goshen was a place of honor and hope. Just when it seemed like the famine may in fact overtake them, God moved in the lives of His people and brought them into something greater than they could have ever even imagined. A place more prosperous than they had ever seen before. Joseph told them that it was a place of protection from poverty. In Goshen they were given the best of the land. All that they had worked for all of their lives could not even compare to what they were given when they entered Goshen. Doesn't that remind you of our good works? Even with all our effort, we could not do for ourselves what God alone can do in a moment.

WE COULD NOT DO FOR
OURSELVES WHAT GOD ALONE
CAN DO IN A MOMENT.

Goshen was also the place of reconciliation for Joseph and his family. It was there that they were able to draw near to one another and make up for the years that had been lost while they were apart from one another. It was a place where what was once estranged was now being brought together in a more wholesome and beautiful way. This time they were a family that loved each other whereas before they were a fractured family full of favorites and rivalries. While Israel did hold fast to Joseph and Benjamin being his favorite sons, because they were birthed from his favored wife; the family was finally whole, together and in unity in the land God had for them. So many parallels to explore concerning Goshen, such as God's people being delivered out of

Egypt in later generations to the Promised Land flowing with milk and honey. Take note that God always has a place of refuge and protection for His people. He will always protect them and deliver them.

So they went up out of Egypt and came to the land of Canaan to their father Jacob. And they told him, "Joseph is still alive, and he is ruler over all the land of Egypt." And his heart became numb, for he did not believe them. But when they told him all the words of Joseph, which he had said to them, and when he saw the wagons that Joseph had sent to carry him, the spirit of their father Jacob revived. And Israel said, "It is enough; Joseph my son is still alive. I will go and see him before I die."

- Genesis 45:25-28

Joseph Brings His Family to Egypt

So Israel took his journey with all that he had and came to Beersheba, and offered sacrifices to the God of his father Isaac. And God spoke to Israel in visions of the night and said, "Jacob, Jacob." And he said, "Here I am." Then he said, "I am God, the God of your father. Do not be afraid to go down to Egypt, for there I will make you into a great nation. I myself will go down with you to Egypt, and I will also bring you up again, and Joseph's hand shall close your eyes."

Then Jacob set out from Beersheba. The sons of
Israel carried Jacob their father, their little ones,
and their wives, in the wagons that Pharaoh had
sent to carry him. They also took their livestock
and their goods, which they had gained in the
land of Canaan, and came into Egypt, Jacob and
all his offspring with him, his sons, and his sons'
sons with him, his daughters, and his sons'
daughters. All his offspring he brought with him
into Egypt. - Genesis 46:1-7

He had sent Judah ahead of him to Joseph to
show the way before him in Goshen, and they
came into the land of Goshen. Then Joseph
prepared his chariot and went up to meet Israel,
his father, in Goshen. He presented himself to
him and fell on his neck and wept on his neck a
good while. Israel said to Joseph, "Now let me
die, since I have seen your face and know that
you are still alive." Joseph said to his brothers
and to his father's household, "I will go up and
tell Pharaoh and will say to him, 'My brothers
and my father's household, who were in the land
of Canaan, have come to me. And the men are
shepherds, for they have been keepers of
livestock, and they have brought their flocks and
their herds and all that they have.' When
Pharaoh calls you and says, 'What is your
occupation?' you shall say, 'Your servants have
been keepers of livestock from our youth even
until now, both we and our fathers,' in order
that you may dwell in the land of Goshen, for

every shepherd is an abomination to the Egyptians." - Genesis 46:28-34

Jacob's Family Settles in Goshen

So Joseph went in and told Pharaoh, "My father and my brothers, with their flocks and herds and all that they possess, have come from the land of Canaan. They are now in the land of Goshen." And from among his brothers he took five men and presented them to Pharaoh. Pharaoh said to his brothers, "What is your occupation?" And they said to Pharaoh, "Your servants are shepherds, as our fathers were." They said to Pharaoh, "We have come to sojourn in the land, for there is no pasture for your servants' flocks, for the famine is severe in the land of Canaan. And now, please let your servants dwell in the land of Goshen." Then Pharaoh said to Joseph,"Your father and your brothers have come to you. The land of Egypt is before you. Settle Your father and your brothers in the best of the land. Let them settle in the land of Goshen, and if you know any able men among them, put them in charge of my livestock."

Then Joseph brought in Jacob his father and stood him before Pharaoh, and Jacob blessed Pharaoh. And Pharaoh said to Jacob, "How many are the days of the years of your life?" And Jacob said to Pharaoh, "The days of the years of my sojourning are 130 years. Few and

evil have been the days of the years of my life, and they have not attained to the days of the years of the life of my fathers in the days of their sojourning." And Jacob blessed Pharaoh and went out from the presence of Pharaoh. Then Joseph settled his father and his brothers and gave them a possession in the land of Egypt, in the best of the land, in the land of Rameses, as Pharaoh had commanded. And Joseph provided his father, his brothers, and all his father's household with food, according to the number of their dependents. - Genesis 47:1-12

Reunited

I am not crying, you are crying! Wow, what a remarkable ending to this story. When Joseph was revealing himself to his brothers he said that while they sold him there, God is who sent him and he sent him ahead of them to preserve their life. He also says that God sent him to preserve for them a remnant on earth. The Twelve Tribes of Israel preserved and reunited once again after years and years of believing that one of the brothers, one of what would become one of the tribes, was dead.

I wonder how many of us could look at the people who sold us out, wanted to kill us and completely let us down and say, "You did not send me here, God did!" Yet the path was not easy, was it? The path was full of hard moments and undeniable sorrow, yet God was in the midst of it all. While there were still five years left in the famine for the rest of the earth, God's people were safe and well supplied for.

Joseph's Dream

Recall with me how this story started, with a dream. When Joseph dreamt that his family was bowing down to him, he could have never fathomed that his dream had almost nothing to do with him and everything to do with God's plan for His people. God has such incredible ways. He uses one life to preserve the entire world through a dream that at the time made very little sense.

The dream had now come to pass and the purpose had now been fulfilled. The stripping of his coat, the pit, the accusations, the prison, the promotion and now finally the purpose were all unveiled for the world to see. While it took Joseph a lifetime to get in position, purpose came in a moment. Sometimes we are in such a hurry to get to the purpose when the positioning is where God has, potentially, the most interest. Sure, God desired to save His people and the entire known world through the life of Joseph, yet if the lifetime of positioning would have been wasted the fulfillment of purpose would have never come.

Consider Noah, he built his entire life for forty days of rain only to spend the rest of his life rebuilding the known world. Moses led the children of Israel out of Egypt, only to die outside of the very Promised Land he was leading them into. Abraham birthed Issac only to die before the entire nation was born through him. Oftentimes we read the lives of the forefathers of our faith and we forget that their natural lives were at times, mundane. We are blessed to know the ins and outs of Joseph's life on many accounts, yet we don't always have such details. Could it be that we at times are so caught in the desire for purpose that we miss it all together by failing to recognize the positioning happening in our midst?

Joseph was finally standing in the fullness of his purpose and he would enjoy the many benefits and blessings that came along with that. What started with just a dream had now been revealed as the very purpose Joseph was born for.

Let's Pray

Father, I praise You, for purpose is only fulfilled through You and through true submission to Your positioning and Your will for our lives. Oh God, like Joseph may I see the fulfillment of the purpose of my life here on this earth. Even if like Abraham and the totality of the purpose is many generations from now, let me see the purpose begin! Let me see Your promises be made manifest here on this earth. I love you, Lord! In Jesus name, amen.

Memory Verse

The land of Egypt is before you. Settle Your father and your brothers in the best of the land. Let them settle in the land of Goshen. (Genesis 47:6)

10

God Meant It For Good

And we know that for those who love God all things work together for good, for those who are called according to his purpose. - Romans 8:28

The doctors kept insisting that I would live, but I knew in my heart they wouldn't tell me if they really thought I was going to die. I mean, why would they? As they wheeled me back in for the emergency surgery that would stop the internal bleeding that had been occurring for eight hours, I could only think of three things; my husband, my daughter, and the books that I did not write. In fact, this book was at the forefront of those thoughts. I wondered if my spiritual daughter who has been editing this book would pick it up and finish it. I wondered if my husband would open my laptop, finish writing it and publish it. I wondered what legacy I had left to raise my daughter in my absence.

I thank God that I did live and I am the one who has the honor of finishing this book. I must admit, my perspective has shifted quite drastically since I started this work four months ago. I assume almost dying would drastically shift anyone's perspective and quickly. When I started writing this book I did so because God had instructed me to, but at the time it did not make sense. To be honest, I was in the toughest ministry season I had ever been in. There were several times while writing this book that I had to stop and weep, because the revelations that I was writing were for far more than just the writing of this book. They were indeed healing my soul as I was processing all that I was standing in. When I began writing this book I was writing from within the middle of the battle, but I can say with full certainty I am finishing it with the victory in hand.

The Day That Changed Everything

God truly is sovereign. When I write my books I lay out the outline before actually writing them. I have the chapters, their corresponding verse and some major outliner thoughts for what that chapter will cover. However, when it came to this book, I had no idea what chapter ten would be about. All I knew was the title would be God Meant It For My Good.

On January 16th, 2023 my husband and I found out that we were pregnant and we were absolutely ecstatic. We have desired another child and our daughter has been eagerly waiting for a sibling. We began the normal pregnancy routine of calling the doctor, getting our first few appointments ready and began researching the latest baby gadgets, but the very next day things changed. I began to have symptoms in my body that I knew were not conducive of a healthy pregnancy.

While I badly wanted to believe that everything would be okay, I knew in my heart that I was miscarrying. A mother knows when something is wrong with her child, even when it is within her and she cannot yet lay her natural eyes on it; she knows. Things escalated quickly as we learned that I had lost the baby and it was stuck in my fallopian tube causing what is called an ectopic pregnancy. Ectopic pregnancies are extremely rare and are the leading cause of maternal death in the first trimester. What makes an ectopic pregnancy so dangerous for the mother is the risk that the tube will rupture causing intense internal bleeding. This can be fatal within hours.

Within minutes of being informed by the doctor that the pregnancy was ectopic, my tube ruptured and I began to bleed internally. Shortly after, I was losing consciousness and screaming in pain. That would have been enough to be scary, but unfortunately my pain was ignored and even shunned by my provider and I was sent home without care; literally dying. After hours of internally bleeding and blacking out, we called 911 and I was rushed to the hospital with no readable blood pressure. I was only hours away from death, but God.

I WAS ONLY HOURS AWAY
FROM DEATH, BUT GOD.

You may wonder how I could possibly sit here and write that God used this terrible situation for my good, but friends the Bible is true all the time! No matter our circumstances. During this internal bleeding, before I received emergency care I hit my garage floor unconscious. We do not know if I blacked out or if I died. All we know is that I was unconscious and completely unresponsive. After my husband desperately tried to pick me up and get me to respond, he did the only thing he knew to do. He looked at my lifeless body on the garage floor and said, "I command you to get up now in the name of Jesus Christ!" Right that second my spirit jolted back into my body and I gasped for air.

Little did my husband know, while I was laying there lifeless my spirit was ascending into heaven. I was more than aware of what was happening, spiritually speaking. I saw the white light, Christ's glory. I was ascending into the glory of the Lord and the most overwhelming part was realizing that He was going to receive me. It reminds me of that song, "still the greatest miracle that I just can't get over, my name is registered in heaven!" I saw the glory of God. His light was the brightest whitest light. You cannot comprehend just how bright His glory was.

When my spirit jolted back into my body and my husband and our associate pastor stood me up to carry me inside my home, I began immediately telling them what I had seen. I even told the doctors what I saw as I was so overcome by the reality of what had taken place. While I still had a recovery journey ahead that included the healing of my physical body, I was marked forever by that moment.

The Unseen is More Real Than The Seen

For our momentary, light distress [this passing trouble] is producing for us an eternal weight of glory [a fullness] beyond all measure [surpassing all comparisons, a transcendent splendor and an endless blessedness]! So we look not at the things which are seen, but at the things which are

unseen; for the things which are visible are temporal [just brief and fleeting], but the things which are invisible are everlasting and imperishable. - 2 Corinthians 4:17-18

That moment produced within me an eternal weight of glory. The revelation that the unseen is more real than the seen will forever mark me. A gift of faith was imparted to me that words fail to carry the weight of. Now, I am more certain than ever that this gospel that we preach is eternal. The angels we see are more real than the couch I am sitting on and the surpassing splendor of our Lord, Jesus Christ, is more real than we can comprehend with our human minds.

Sure, I believed before, afterall I was ascending into His glory to be received into eternity with Him. Yet the certainty that I have now is very different. My faith now is greater than I ever thought possible. The conviction I speak with, the authority I walk in, it has all increased and grown. Strength came not only to my mortal body as I healed, but also to my faith and my spirit man.

God did not allow this tragedy to remain as just a loss to me and our family, but rather He turned even the mourning around and caused the scariest moments of my life to also become the most profound and life changing. Like Joseph, while what happened to me from the outside looking in may seem to have been a pit, a stripping of my covering, a valley or prison moment, it has propelled me forward in ways that only God can explain.

Valleys Produce

I want to encourage you that God can and will do the very same for you, no matter what you are facing. The momentary afflictions can and will produce within us an eternal weight of glory, if we let them. Imagine if after Joseph's brothers came he began chastising them and rebuking them for what they had done to him. He would certainly not have been in the wrong had he done that, but rather he had allowed God to refine him; redefine him even. He had allowed God to use all the things that had gone "wrong" in his life to produce within him a greatness that the mountaintop cannot produce.

My husband recently preached an incredible sermon on the mountain and the valley. Something he said will stay with me forever. He spoke of the fruits of the spirit and how we are to grow and mature in them. He then explained that fruits cannot grow on the very tops of mountains. Few things, even wildlife can live at the very top of high altitude mountains. Fruits are grown in valleys, Goshens that are suitable for crops and livestock. He likewise explained that some fruits only grow from pits such as cherries and avocados.

Trials in This Life

Beloved, do not be surprised at the fiery trial when it comes upon you to test you, as though something strange were happening to you. 13 But rejoice insofar as you share Christ's sufferings, that you may also rejoice and be glad when his glory is revealed. - 1 Peter 4:12-13

Friends, we will face trials in this life; that is promised, but it is what we allow the trials to produce within us that matters. God's promises are sure, they are trustworthy and true. He will use all things together for our good. There is this idea with charismatic circles that we will never endure trial or hardship in this life, so when such things happen we begin to question God and our faith as a whole. Yet that idea is not founded in the truth of God's word. Yes, there are things that we do to safeguard ourselves from the wiles of the devil and even the effects of sin on this earth, yet Apostle Paul said clearly do not be surprised by these things as though something strange were happening to you. Apostle Paul said we ought to rejoice! That sounds absolutely absurd if you do not have revelation that trials produce.

Look at how every trial produced positioning with Joseph until his purpose was fulfilled. Trials truly expose to both us, God, and those around us where our faith and trust truly lies. If our faith truly lies in God alone and we believe His Word, not even the hardest trial we could ever face can knock us off course. Though I stared death in its face, I not only lived to tell the tale, but I arose with victory greater than I ever had before. I do not sit here and write this from a place of trauma or even mourning, though I did mourn the loss of my unborn child for a time. I sit here writing this just seven weeks after almost dying with a faith that causes mountains to crumble into the sea.

I sit here with a revelation on the unseen that I would not have received had I not sought God in the midst of my trial. While I was sitting on my couch healing from the surgery, I listened to anointed teaching on faith. I refused to let my faith waiver even in the midst of what I was facing. Yes, moments were tough, but friends when we truly commit every detail of our lives to God not a single moment or trial is wasted.

You Have Been Positioned for Purpose

It is time that the trials in your life produce fully. It is time for you to understand the positioning that has taken place and be prepared for the purpose when it comes. If we fail to understand the positioning, we will fail to recognize the purpose. You have within you greatness, steadfastness, strength and vigor. For all of your life God has been positioning for you for a purpose. I dare you to give thought to the overview of your life and find the hidden timeline that God has woven within. I believe that you will be shocked to find that your life is a message to the world. A message that you have simply yet to fully detect.

You and I, my friend, are in many ways just like Joseph; being positioned for purpose.

Bibliography

"DICTIONARY.COM." Collins English Dictionary - Complete & Unabridged 2012 Digital Edition. January 5, 2023. https://www.dictionary.com/browse/goshen.

Hirsch, G. Emil and J. F. McLaughlin. "Potiphar or Poti-ferah." *Jewish Encyclopedia*, 1906. https://www.jewishencyclopedia.com/articles/12316-potiphar. Accessed 22 Nov. 2022.

Rendsburg, Gary. "YHWH's War Against the Egyptian Sun-God Ra." *The Torah*, 2022. https://www.thetorah.com/article/yhwhs-war-against-the-egyptian-sun-god-ra.

Made in the USA
Coppell, TX
30 December 2023

27085381R00085